REVERSIBLE
SCARVES

REVERSIBLE SCARVES

Curing the Wrong Side Blues

AUDREY KNIGHT

AudKnits, LLC
Paso Robles, California
www.AudKnits.com

Second Edition

Published by AudKnits, LLC
www.audknits.com

Senior Editor: Shannon Okey
Assistant Editor: Elizabeth Green Musselman
Technical Editors: Elizabeth Sullivan, Tana Pageler

Models: Kim Andersen, Dean Brockert, Melanie Brockert, Mallory Caloca, Karen Clark, Alana Dakos, Danielle Dugan, Steve Ells, Jim Gilletly, Audrey Knight, Elisa McNamara, Stitchy McYarnpants, Kellee Middlebrooks, Stephanie Pajonas, Jackie Pawlowski, Joelle Riffle, David Stensland, Connor Storlie, Mel Vassey, Ann Weaver, Pamela Wynne

ISBN 13: 978-0-9887195-2-1

Originally published by Cooperative Press

To my mother, Lucia, whose many talents and kindness continue to inspire me, and to my husband Steve, whose encouragement and faith in me mean everything.

TABLE OF CONTENTS

INTRODUCTION AND TECHNIQUES

CHAPTER 1: DECISIONS, DECISIONS

CHAPTER 2: SURPRISINGLY SIMPLE STITCHES

CHAPTER 3: MULTI-YARN MARVELS

CHAPTER 4: CABLES AND RIBS IN REVERSE

CHAPTER 5: TWICE THE FUN WITH DOUBLE-KNITTING

CHAPTER 6: LUSCIOUS LACINESS

INTRODUCTION AND TECHNIQUES

I remember as a new knitter making a lovely ribbed lace scarf for my friend Margaret. I pored through beautiful patterns and delectable yarns, finally choosing just the right combination to fit her style. Little did I know that when the scarf was complete, it would look beautiful on only one side. Adding to my dismay, it curled in on itself; not even the most careful blocking cured the problem. When Margaret tied it around her neck, the unattractive "wrong" side faced forward.

This started my quest for scarf patterns that don't have a wrong side and that lie flat. This book, *Reversible Scarves: Curing the Wrong Side Blues*, shows you what I've learned on that quest. This is the book I wish I'd had on my knitting bookshelf over the years.

Scarves are blank canvases waiting for color, texture, and pleasing stitch patterns. For most of us, scarves are a big part of our repertoire when we first learn to knit. The simple, rectangular shapes and repetitive patterns offer a wonderful way to master the basics. As we become more proficient, we revisit scarves often. They make marvelous gifts; they're a great way to try new yarns and new stitch patterns; and they can be comforting buddies while we travel. By choosing the perfect color, the right yarn weight, and a plain or fancy pattern, we can easily create just the right accent to an outfit that's hanging in our closet.

In short, scarves are a versatile and fun part of our knitting bags – from our first days of picking up the needles, straight on through decades of knitting.

This book remedies the problem of finding reversible, lay-flat patterns. All in one place, you'll discover designs that range from simple ribs to more complex double knitting. Before you launch into your project, you need to consider who you're making the scarf for. A man? A woman? Is she an urban sophisticate, or maybe a young student? Is this for a friend who needs a warm scarf for hiking, or for navigating New York on a blustery morning? In Chapter 1, "Decisions, Decisions," I use a simple Mistake Stitch Rib pattern to introduce beginners to considerations they need to think about when creating that perfect scarf.

New knitters will find that they can make stunning creations out of deceptively easy patterns such as those found in the "Surprisingly Simple Stitches" chapter. Intermediate knitters will delight in the variety of patterns in the "Cables & Reversible Ribs" and "Luscious Lace" chapters. Even advanced knitters may find patterns that challenge them with a skill they haven't tried before, such as double knitting.

Tips that will encourage you to make your own creations are sprinkled throughout the book. Some patterns include photos of alternative yarn choices so you'll be inspired to try a variety of yarns. And "Make It Your Own" sidebars give you hints about making your own designs from scratch. Finally, I give you even more ideas for customizing scarf patterns by showing you how easily I turned a scarf pattern into a wrap. I hope you will find "Reversible Scarves" a book to turn to for years to come, trying out different patterns as the mood strikes, or as inspiration to design your own.

ABOUT THE PATTERNS: A LITTLE UNCONVENTIONAL

Sometimes the "right" way a pattern is written drives me crazy. I know, I know: the patterns we see in print are often constrained by space, but I find they can be concise to the point of annoyance. Sometimes there isn't enough information for me to be able to easily substitute yarns. Or maybe there's a lot of jumping back and forth in the instructions, with "Repeat row a, repeat row x, repeat row…" You probably know what I mean. Jumping back and forth, I easily lose my place.

In *Reversible Scarves*, I've set out to make the patterns as user-friendly as possible. Here are my breaks with convention:

1. Where possible, I've written longer patterns that don't make you jump back and forth. Call them "Sticky-Note Friendly" if you will. In the written instructions, where possible, I wrote out repeated lines instead of saying "repeat row x." This way, you can move your place marker step by step down the pattern, without those annoying "repeat row xyz" that cause you to stop and have to bounce to some other part of the pattern, execute the repeat, and then bounce back

again. Where I have absolutely had to put a "repeat" instruction in, I've given you rows and charts to follow, which will keep the instructions clear. I hope you find my patterns relaxing to make.

2. Where possible, I use stockinette for the pattern's gauge requirements. There were some cases, though, where that didn't make sense to me, for example in stitch patterns like the linen stitch or lace patterns where knitters' tension or blocking make a big difference.

3. In the description of the yarn, I include the stitch gauge from the ball band. I also include estimated yardage for you home-spun enthusiasts. I hope this'll make it easy for you to substitute yarns.

4. I've seen many a knitter drive herself to distraction when she gets the stitch gauge, but the row gauge just won't quite match. For patterns where the row count isn't important to the outcome, I don't include it in the gauge.

To add to your knitting enjoyment, I've also included some helpful tips in the "Charts," "Lace" and "Nifty Little Tips" sections of the Techniques chapter.

TECHNIQUES

SWATCHING

Is it really necessary to knit a gauge swatch for a scarf? Well, no. After all, it doesn't have to fit "just so," as does a sweater. Whether you make a swatch depends on whether you're like me… before I commit to a project, I want to have an idea of how it's going to look. I would hate to make an entire scarf, only to realize at the end that it would have looked better just a needle size up or down, for example.

Swatches can be really helpful, too, for things like testing the cast-on and bind-off for a lengthwise scarf. I remember the first time I made a lengthwise scarf; I bought some beautiful yarn, cast on hundreds of stitches, spent several days knitting those long, long rows, only to find out that my cast-on was a smidge too tight, causing the edge to bow in. I wasted all that time, when a good-sized swatch would have taught me how loose the cast-on needed to be.

I like to keep the swatches I make. Some are inspired by designs in stitch dictionaries; the ones that don't immediately work out often find their way into other projects later on. An added bonus to swatching is that I always learn something useful about the yarn I'm working with. For example, the first time I made a swatch from bamboo I was happily surprised to see how beautifully it draped! As a designer, it helps me to make a list of the gauges I get with different yarns. I even have software that helps me keep track. When I want a yarn substitute, or need a reminder of what needle I get gauge with in a particular yarn, I can easily look it up. Check out the "Resources" section at the end of the book if you're interested in the swatch software I use.

CASTING ON AND BINDING OFF

There are plenty of good resources for learning the most common cast-on techniques, such as long-tail, knitting-on, and cable. In this section I give you food for thought for taking these techniques a bit further. If you're like me and appreciate the finished look of an edge bound off in pattern, how do you cast on to match? What special considerations might you want to think about when casting on large numbers of stitches for a vertical scarf? And finally, what are some tips for binding off? And then there's the endearing, intriguing Moebius. It gets its own set of cast-on instructions.

CASTING ON IN PATTERN

I enjoy a good edge. When a project ends with the instructions "bind off in pattern," I know that the end of my work will include a sequence of knit and purl stitches. I want my cast-on to match the bind-off so that both ends of my project look similar. This blissful symmetry comes about through the use of purled, as well as knit, cast-on stitches. I'm assuming you already know how to cast on using the basic long-tail and knitted cast-on methods. Here's how to cast on purlwise in both:

LONG-TAIL PURL CAST-ON: Hold yarn as you would for standard long-tail cast-on, with a loop of yarn around the index finger and a loop around the thumb. Bring the needle toward the far side of the yarn, coming up under and hooking the far finger strand (figs. A & B).

Bring the needle above the near strand of the finger loop. Dip it under the far strand of the thumb loop, hooking the strand (fig. C). Draw hooked thumb strand from front to back through the finger loop (fig. D).

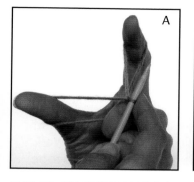 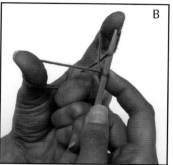 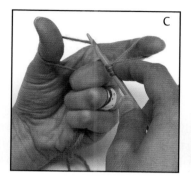 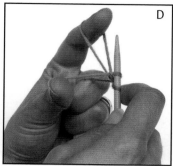

PURLED-ON CAST-ON: This is worked just like the knitted cast-on, but instead of knitting into the left-hand needle stitch, you will be purling into it.

Bring the right-hand needle through the stitch as if to purl (fig. E); leave the old stitch on the left-hand needle and the newly formed stitch on the right-hand needle. Wrap the right-hand needle as you would for a purl stitch (fig. F); pull the new "stitch" out to the right a bit (fig. G).

With the tip of the left-hand needle, dip below the new stitch with the left-hand needle, then upward through the stitch, slipping it onto the left-hand needle (fig. H).

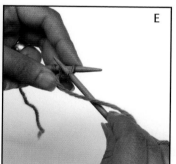 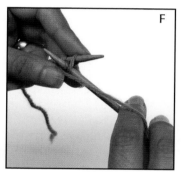 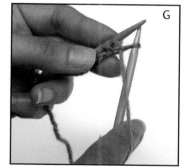 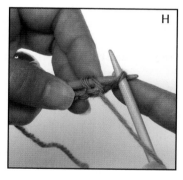

The trick to matching a combination of knit/purl cast-on stitches is to think about whether the cast-on is going to be seen from the right side or wrong side of the work.

To wrap my head around how to cast on in pattern, I always grab a piece of graph or plain paper and draw the first row, adding a row for the cast-on below it. Let's say Row 1 in the pattern is on the right side (RS) of the work, and you want your cast-on to match the first row. If you're using the long-tail method, your cast-on is seen from the wrong side. To work the pattern's first row, you turn the work. This means that your cast-on knit/purl combination will be the opposite of the pattern's first row. Simply cast on just as you would work any wrong-side row, where you purl the wrong-side stitches that read as knit on the right side, and knit the wrong-side stitches that read as purls on the right side. Let's say the pattern's first row is a right-side row calling for k3, p4, k2. This is the right side of the work. Working from the wrong side, it would be p2, k4, p3. This is the stitch combination you will use, then, to cast on using long-tail knit/purl.

On the other hand, a knitted cast-on is seen from the right side of the work. Taking the same stitch pattern of k3, p4, k2, the stitches will need to be cast on by knitting on 2 stitches, purling on 4 stitches, then knitting on 3 stitches. In both the cast-on and the first row, the k2 stitches are closest to the blunt end of the needle.

By casting on your project in a knit/purl sequence that matches the pattern, you can achieve a polished edge that will match other end of the scarf when it's bound off in pattern.

BINDING OFF

When a project ends in a stitch pattern, I love to bind off in pattern. Especially when paired with a cast-on in pattern, the ends mirror each other nicely. Usually, I bind off with the same needle that I've used for the rest of the pattern. Sometimes, though, a larger needle gives me better results for a more uniform edge, or one that needs to stretch out. I use my gauge swatch to figure out ahead of time what needle size to use.

SCARVES WORKED LENGTHWISE

Scarves that are worked lengthwise require more careful planning than scarves worked back-and-forth across the width. Casting on a large number of stitches can be tricky; little errors in tension become magnified over long distances. Work that cast-on too tightly, and your edge will bow in; work it too loosely and your edge will ruffle. There are decisions to be made about which cast-on method to use, as there are advantages to each.

CABLE CAST-ON

This cast-on doesn't produce as stretchy an edge as the long-tail method, but it's easier to get more uniform tension across long distances. It can produce an end that looks loose. For the first row after this cast-on, I typically knit through the back loops (tbl) to tighten the stitches.

Alternatively, for self–fringing scarves where the yarn is cut at the end of each row and the pattern is in garter stitch, I like to slide the stitches to the other end of the circular needle, then turn the work, to begin the pattern so the bumpier side faces out, just as it would if it were part of the garter stitch pattern.

Finally, I like the cable cast-on for large numbers of stitches since it takes the guess work out of the length of yarn needed.

THE LONG-TAIL METHOD

While this book assumes you already know the more basic long-tail and knitted cast-ons, I do want to discuss how to use them in scarves. The long-tail cast-on is my favorite, but it can be a challenge to get the tension right where a large number of stitches is involved.

If you want to use this cast-on, I suggest making a sizeable swatch first so you can determine the best tension to give you a flat edge. While some knitters use a larger needle size to avoid the cast-on edge pulling inward, the ideal method is to space the stitches out enough. This prevents the larger loop that forms when using a larger needle.

A big consideration in using the long-tail cast-on lengthwise is how to keep from running out of yarn before the cast-on is finished. Where do you put the slip knot to avoid running out of yarn? There are several methods you can use.

You can estimate the yardage needed by casting on a small number of stitches, then measuring the length of yarn used, extrapolating for the length required for the entire cast-on, and adding an additional length for the tail.

Let's say the pattern calls for casting on 300 stitches. Loosely cast 10 stitches onto the needle you used to obtain gauge. Mark the point at which the tail end of the yarn is close to the needle. Pull the stitches off the needle and measure the length between the slip knot and the point you marked. Let's say you get 6." Since you ultimately need 300 stitches cast on, you know you'll need 30 times the length of yarn used for 10 stitches, or 30 x 6" = 180." Adding in 10" for a tail to weave in, you would figure 180" + 10" = 190" or about 5.3 yards for the cast-on.

A trick I learned from *Lily Chin's Knitting Tips & Tricks: Shortcuts and Techniques Every Knitter Should Know* for estimating the yardage needed for a long-tail cast-on is to start with a tail that is three times the length of the scarf, plus 10%. If the scarf from the first example is 60" long, multiply 60" x 3 = 180". Adding in an additional 10%, the calculation ends up as 180" + (180 x .1), that is, 180" + 18 = 198". Finally, add 6" for the tail for 5.5 yards.

Or you can use two balls of yarn, avoiding the possibility of running out. Tie the cast-on's slip knot using the ends of both balls of yarn. Hold the strands as you normally would for the long-tail cast-on. Once you've cast on the required number of stitches, cut the second strand of yarn, leaving a tail to weave in later. Proceed as usual with the remaining ball of yarn.

KNITTED- OR PURLED-ON METHOD

As with the chain cast-on, the knitted-on or purled-on cast on has the advantage of being worked on the same size needle as the rest of the scarf; it is easier to maintain the correct tension; and there is no worry about running out of yarn. It is not my favorite cast-on for most purposes, as it leaves a loose edge.

COUNTING MADE EASY!

When casting on a large number of stitches, I like to place a stitch marker every 20 stitches. This keeps me from having to count and re-count scores and – worse – hundreds of the same stitches over and over. Ugh!

Instead, I cast on 20 stitches, counting again for accuracy, and then place a marker. I do the same with the next 20 stitches and the next until I have all the multiples of 20 that will fit into the required number of cast-on stitches. Even better, before I start casting on I put out the number of stitch markers I'll need.

Say I want to cast on 272 stitches like in the Shading Stripes pattern. I know that 20 goes into 272 13 times, with 12 stitches left over. I get 13 stitch markers out, knowing that when I've used all of them up, it's time to count the final 12 stitches. For me, this method makes casting on mindless, which means I can do more enjoyable things like listen to my favorite knitting podcasts as I cast on.

CROSSED STITCHES

The C2F and C2B crossed stitches found in the Wavy pattern are good examples of small cables that can be knit without using a cable needle. To watch how these are made, look for my AudKnits how-to video "Knitting: Cables Without a Cable Needle" on YouTube: http://youtu.be/dT84v90Lc_I

C2F (CROSS 2 FRONT): Skip the first st on the left-hand needle and knit the second st though the back loop and leave it on the needle (figs. A & B below).

Twist the right-hand needle to the front of the work and knit the skipped st through the front loop (fig. C). Slip both sts off the needle (fig. D).

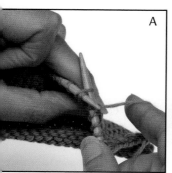  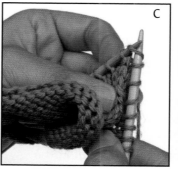 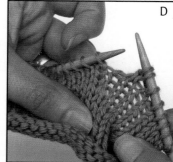

C2B (CROSS 2 BACK): Skip the first stitch on the left-hand needle and knit the second stitch through the front loop (figs. E & F).

Leaving the stitch on the needle, knit the skipped st through the front loop (fig. G). Then slip both sts off the needle together (fig. H).

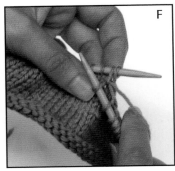
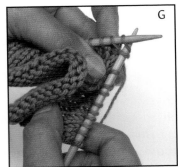

MOEBIUS CAST-ON

The cast-on for a Moebius seems tricky at first, but is well worth learning. I was surprised at how little time it took to become familiar with it. I learned this method from Cat Bordhi and am grateful to her for her excellent teaching style! Cat Bordhi's terrific video demonstrating the Moebius Cast-On technique can be found here: http://youtu.be/LVnTda7F2V4.

For this cast-on, you will use a very long circular needle. The knitting is worked with the needle cable coiled onto itself. For a 30" scarf, for example, you'll need to use a 47" circular needle, as the length is only about 23" once it's doubled over. When working a Moebius project, you're working stitches from both coils of the needle, so you still need the same number of stitches that the 30" scarf would normally require. It's easy to cast on too loosely, so I suggest making your cast-on stitches snug. Here's how to cast on:

1. Make a slip knot, leaving enough tail for weaving in later. Slip the knot to the middle of the cable (fig. A).
2. Make a coil in the cable by bringing the left needle counter-clockwise around in a circle, holding it against the slip knot still in the center of the cable. The needle points to the left (fig. B).
3. Hold the needle in your right hand, while also grasping the slip knot and cable. Tension the working yarn over your left index finger while pinching the cable between thumb and middle finger, about 3" from the slip knot. A triangle is formed by your left hand as one leg, the yarn as the right leg, and the cable as the base. This is the set up to start casting on (fig. C).

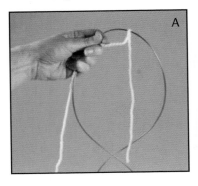
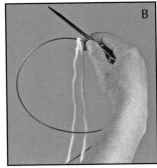
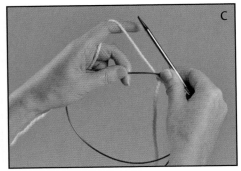

4. The stitches are cast onto the cable and then the needle, alternating. Work the stitches snugly. To form the cable stitches, point the needle toward you, bring it down and away from you under the cable. Bring the needle upward between the cable and yarn (fig. D).
5. Bring needle up over the top of the yarn, pointing away from you. Draw the yarn downward, then toward you under the cable. You will have hooked the yarn and brought it forward under the needle (fig. E).

6. Bring needle back above the cable, so the stitch looks like a little triangle, with the cable forming the bottom leg. This is your cable stitch (fig. F).

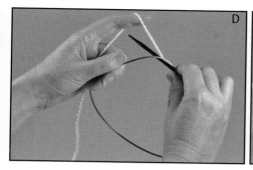 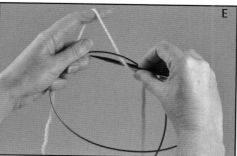 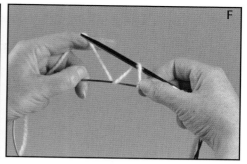

7. The next stitch will be a needle stitch. Still holding the yarn up with your left index finger, and keeping the needle above the cable, bring the needle up over the top of the yarn, then to the back, catching the yarn as you bring the needle toward you, forming a simple yarnover. This first needle stitch counts as your first cast-on stitch (fig. G).
8. Counting: Count only the stitches above the cable. Do not count the slip knot. I highly recommend having a little pile of locking stitch markers at hand, placing one after every 20 or 50 counted stitches to more easily keep track of the total. I like the locking stitch markers that are big enough not to slip under the yarnover-type stitch formed in Step 7 above. Remove them only when you're sure you've cast on the required number of stitches (fig. H).

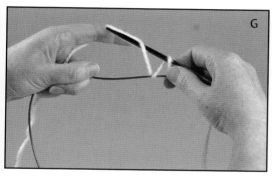 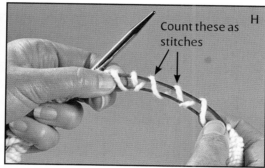

Count these as stitches

9. Continue adding stitches using steps 4-7 until you've cast on the required number of stitches.
10. Bring the unused needle around clockwise to meet up with the cast on needle; gently pull the cable so the two circles formed are about equal length (fig. I).
11. Spread stitches out until the slip knot is near the tip of the left needle (the formerly unused needle). The first and last cast-on stitches are near each other. You'll notice the slip knot is now the first stitch on the left needle (fig. J).
12. Put the work down on a flat surface and make sure the cables parallel each other until they cross once at the end. It is important that there is only one "crossing" (a sort of half-twist) in the cast-on (fig. K).

 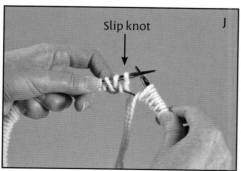 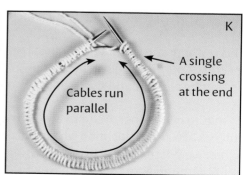

Slip knot

Cables run parallel

A single crossing at the end

13. As in circular knitting, place a marker on the right needle to indicate the beginning of a round.

14. The slip knot is the first stitch on the left needle; work it as you would the first stitch in any knitting. One Moebius round consists of working around both rings formed by the coiled cable, and is complete when you reach the marker.

15. On the first half of the round, up to where the stitch marker is below your needles (marking the halfway point), the cast-on stitches will not look the same; alternately, the right leg of one goes behind the needle, while the right leg of the next goes in front of the needle. Work them all the same way, inserting your right needle into the triangle formed by the cable as the base, and the yarn as the two sides (fig. L).

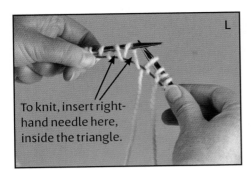

To knit, insert right-hand needle here, inside the triangle.

CHARTS

The charts in this book are worked from the bottom up. For flat knitting, odd rows are worked from right to left, and even rows are worked from left to right.

Each symbol represents the way the knitting looks facing you. It takes just a small amount of practice to get used to remembering that a knit symbol on the chart is worked as a knit stitch on the odd rows (the "right" side of the work), and is purled on the even rows (the "wrong" side of the work) so that it appears as a knit stitch on the "right" side. Patterns worked in the round are even easier, since all the stitches in the chart are worked from right to left, and all stitches face the knitter.

My favorite tool for working with charts is sticky notes. You can get them in various widths, depending on the width of the chart. Apply the sticky note just above the chart line you're currently working on. This keeps track of which row or round you're on, hides the rows you don't yet need, and allows you to see the rows below it that you've already worked. That way, if a purl stitch is supposed to be worked directly above a knit stitch, for instance, you can see right away if you're off track.

LACE

I don't think anyone knits lace without making mistakes along the way. You can either find the mistake after several rows and have to rip back, or you can count stitches as you go. I like to count as I go, even if it seems tedious. For me, ripping back lace and then having to figure out which row I'm on is worse than counting all the stitches in every row.

This is where stitch markers come in handy. Using charts, it's easy to figure out how many stitches should be between the markers. Counting the stitches between the markers, as opposed to across a whole row, goes relatively quickly. (When the beginning of the round shifts, you may have to move the pattern repeat markers as well.)

Thanks to my teacher Brenda, I always use a lifeline. When things go really wrong, the lifeline holds a row or round of stitches at a known location which you can rip back to if necessary. To make a lifeline, take some smooth waste yarn (in a lighter weight than the yarn you're using) or dental floss and thread it through the stitches on your needle. Choosing a row/round without increases, decreases, or yarnovers is best. Be sure to go around the outside of the stitch markers, not through them, or you won't be able to move them up to the next row! Mark on your chart or in the instructions which row you put the lifeline in so you can easily go back to it if needed. If you do end up ripping back to the lifeline, when working the next row be careful not to knit the lifeline into the stitch. Every so often as you progress in the pattern, give your work a close look and make sure everything looks accurate, then move the lifeline up. Even if I'm counting, I've made mistakes or dropped stitches and had to rip back to the lifeline, which made it well worth the effort of putting it in.

If you are as bad as I am at multi-tasking, you may want to save your lace knitting for quiet times without distraction. I've learned through experience that I simply cannot knit lace while knitting with my friends. I always keep a simpler project on hand for social knitting.

WEAVING IN ENDS

Hiding the tails of yarn in reversible knitting can take a bit more forethought and care than in regular knitting, where we can hide the ends on the "wrong" side or in seams. There are several good places to weave in ends that will be inconspicuous on either side.

At the ends of the scarf, I find it very easy and almost invisible to weave the end in along the bottom cast-on and top bind-off edges. I just make sure I leave a longer tail than usual so I have plenty to weave in across the entire end (fig. A).

Another useful technique is the duplicate stitch. If you're weaving in an end from the edge of your work, thread a tapestry needle and follow like-colored stitches just as you would for duplicate stitches (fig B).

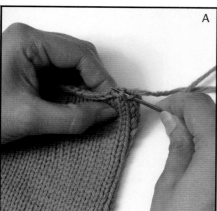 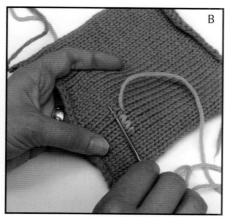

If you're using this method when joining yarns in the middle of a row, make sure to weave the two yarn ends in the direction they were originally traveling, which will be in opposite directions to each other. In other words, you want to make sure that where the two yarns meet, they don't make a hole. Thread a tapestry needle, and bringing the tail across the area where the two yarns meet, follow the stitches just as you would when adding a decorative duplicate stitch.

NIFTY LITTLE TIPS

Here are some little snippets of advice that make my knitting life easier, and I hope will do the same for you:

- It can be confusing to figure out whether the work that's facing you is the right side or wrong side. I like to use my cast-on tail as a reference. I jot down on my pattern whether the tail is on the bottom right or bottom left corner of the piece when the right side is facing me.
- The other option is to use a locking stitch marker, and just attach it to the right side of the work, moving the marker up the work as necessary so you can see it at a glance. Again, if you're like me, it'll be helpful to jot down on the pattern which side the marker indicates.
- When I first learned to knit, in my eagerness to start a new pattern, I'd just delve right in – a reckless move as it turned out. After getting hopelessly lost and spending time and money on disasters, I learned that in the end I'm much happier if I read through the entire pattern before starting it.
- I check online for errata before I begin knitting from a pattern.
- As I read through a new pattern, I highlight or underline little – but important – instructions that I know will be easily missed, such as "at the same time," "on larger needle," or "wyib."

I hope that the special techniques and tips presented here give you new tools to use in all your knitting, and especially help you to achieve beautiful results in making your reversible scarves.

CHAPTER 1: DECISIONS, DECISIONS

Some knitters like to make patterns exactly as they appear in the pattern's photograph, using the same yarn and color. If you're one of those people, you may want to skip right to one of the patterns in this book. Or maybe you're someone who views a pattern as a jumping off point. You may want to alter the size, color, or texture to achieve a different look for your own wardrobe or a friend's.

If you want ideas for how to tailor your scarf to match the personality and lifestyle of the person you're making it for, this chapter is for you.

CHOOSING YARN

Although I'm no longer a beginning knitter, I can still feel overwhelmed when I walk into my local yarn store to select yarn for a scarf. I tend to get distracted, fall in love with every fiber I see, and want to take ALL the yarn home with me.

I find it helpful to think about my project ahead of time so that I can focus on a few key characteristics when I step into that den of temptation, the yarn shop.

One of the joys – and challenges – of knitting is matching the look of your project to its recipient. Here are the kinds of questions a knitter should ask herself when making any of the scarves in this book:

- Who am I knitting this scarf for? Is it for a man? Does he like a tailored look? If so, a heathery DK weight may be just the ticket. Or is he more the rugged type, in which case the worsted tweed version might be a good choice. Is the scarf for a woman? Is her style hip or laid back or refined? City or country? A bright chunky yarn lends a casual look, while an airy mohair can glam it up for a night on the town.

- Consider the scarf's use and the season it'll be worn in. Is it functional, needing to keep the wearer warm in arctic conditions? Then you'll want to make the scarf wide and out of a fiber that will retain warmth. Is it mostly decorative? The finer yarn of a sport-weight version may add just the right touch to a bright spring outfit.

- What about color? Will your scarf accent an outfit, or be the center of attention? A spring accessory might be the color of new blossoms. In winter, you might want to use subdued colors that will go with the browns, blacks and grays common to cold-weather wear. Or maybe it's a chance to add a punch of color to a dreary winter.

- Does the scarf need to be easy to wash? In that case, look for superwash wools. If the scarf will be lovingly hand washed (maybe by you?), your options widen to include all sorts of fibers, from luxurious cashmere to cool cotton or bamboo.

ONE PATTERN, SIX WAYS: VARYING YOUR SCARF'S LOOK WITH MISTAKE STITCH RIBS

When I was new to knitting, it amazed me to see the variety of looks that my fellow knitters could coax out of just one pattern. Seeing the results that can be achieved by altering the yarn's weight, texture, dimensions, and color helped me to visualize changes I could make in future projects. The Mistake Stitch Ribs scarf instructions that begin on the next page will help you explore some of the infinite possibilities contained in just one pattern.

To help get you started in thinking about your scarf project, I've used the popular Mistake Stitch Rib to illustrate the different looks you can achieve by changing up yarn weights, colors, and dimensions. From rugged to refined, from brightly saturated to calmly muted, this simple pattern can serve up just the right combination. The stitch is easy to memorize, lies flat, and is (of course!) reversible.

I show off the Mistake Stitch Rib's versatility here, with six different weights of yarn. Look through the variations to get inspiration for your own creations. Then apply the "Pattern Basics" to your choice of yarn.

THE PATTERN BASICS

Apply these basic instructions to the yarn weight you choose for your scarf, using the dimensions, gauges, and cast-on numbers as a guide to make your own. See the following pages for details on using different yarn weights with this basic pattern.

Mistake Stitch Rib:
Cast on a multiple of 4 sts plus 3. If you want to make your bottom edge match your top edge, try casting on in pattern (see the Techniques chapter for instructions).

Using the long-tail method, * cast on 2 sts knitwise, cast on 2 sts purlwise; rep from * to last 3 sts, cast on 2 knitwise sts, cast on 1 st purlwise.

Row 1: * K2, p2; rep from * to last 3 sts, k2, p1.
Repeat this row to desired length.

Bind off in pattern. Weave in ends (see the Techniques chapter for how to weave in ends so they don't show).

SPORT WEIGHT VERSION

A fine weight yarn creates a pretty accessory – here, made as an accent piece for young woman who enjoys her garden. It's perfect as a gift in spring. The machine-washable yarn makes it easy for a busy gal to take care of her scarf.

FINISHED MEASUREMENTS

4" x 62"/10cm x 157.5cm

YARN

Lorna's Laces Shepherd Sport (100% superwash wool; 200 yd/183m per 70g skein) (for substitution purposes, 24 sts = 4"/10cm as per ball band); color: #40ns, Sunshine; 2 skeins.

Or approximately 300 yards of sport weight yarn.

NEEDLES & NOTIONS

1 pair US #4/3.5mm straight needles
Tapestry needle

GAUGE

35 sts = 4"/10cm in pattern stitch, after blocking with ribbing slightly stretched

PATTERN

Cast on 35 sts in pattern.
Follow instructions in "Pattern Basics" above.

DK WEIGHT VERSION

A versatile weight, DK looks good in skinny, wide or in between. Shown here in a heather color for an urban flair. Machine washability is an especially welcome choice for a man.

FINISHED MEASUREMENTS
6" x 72"/15cm x 183cm

YARN
Knit Picks Swish DK (100% superwash merino wool; 123 yds/112m per 50g ball) (for substitution purposes, 22 sts = 4"/10cm as per ball band); color: #24312, Delft Heather; 6 balls.

Or approximately 615 yards of DK weight yarn.

NEEDLES & NOTIONS
1 pair US #4/3.5mm straight needles
Tapestry needle

GAUGE
31 sts = 4"/10cm in pattern stitch, after blocking with ribbing slightly stretched

PATTERN
Cast on 35 sts in pattern.
Follow instructions in "Pattern Basics" on page 20.

A COMPLETELY DIFFERENT TAKE ON DK - MOHAIR

A fuzzy mohair creates a whole new look for this scarf. This one is light, airy, sophisticated and feminine – just right for an elegant night out. Made shorter, it's just right for tucking into a winter coat.

FINISHED MEASUREMENTS
7.5" x 40"/19cm x 101.5cm

YARN
GGH Soft-Kid (70% super kid mohair, 25% nylon, 5% wool; 150 yd/137m per 25g ball) (for substitution purposes, 18 sts = 4"/10cm as per ball band); color: #055, Light Pink; 2 balls.

Or approximately 240 yards of DK weight mohair yarn.

NEEDLES & NOTIONS
1 pair #US 8/5mm straight needles
Tapestry needle

GAUGE
23 sts = 4"/10 cm in pattern stitch, after blocking with ribbing slightly stretched

PATTERN
Cast on 43 sts in pattern.
Follow instructions in "Pattern Basics" on page 20.

WORSTED WEIGHT VERSION

A tweed texture is a good match for an outdoorsy sort of person. A worsted weight yarn makes for a warm scarf that is just right for cold weather.

FINISHED MEASUREMENTS
8" x 70"/20.5cm x 178cm

YARN
Debbie Bliss Donegal Luxury Tweed Aran (85% baby wool, 15% angora; 96 yd/88m per 50g ball) (for substitution purposes, 18 sts = 4"/10cm as per ball band); color: #360014, Chocolate; 6 balls.

Or approximately 450 yards of worsted weight yarn.

NEEDLES & NOTIONS
1 pair US #8/5mm straight needles
Tapestry needle

GAUGE
25 sts = 4"/10cm in pattern stitch, after blocking with ribbing slightly stretched

PATTERN
Cast on 47 sts in pattern.
Follow instructions in "Pattern Basics" on page 20.

BULKY WEIGHT VERSION

This version of the mistake rib scarf is knit wide and in a lofty alpaca for serious fall and winter warmth. Tone-on-tone yarn lends interest without being too busy. (A closeup of this scarf is shown on page 27.)

FINISHED MEASUREMENTS

6.5" x 60"/16.5cm x 152.5cm

YARN

Misti Alpaca Tonos Chunky (50% baby alpaca, 50% merino wool; 109 yd/100m per 100g skein) (for substitution purposes, 14 sts = 4"/10cm as per ball band); color: #TTC06, Grassroots; 2 skeins for 55"/139.5cm length or less, 3 skeins for more than 55"/139.5cm.

Or approximately 230 yards of bulky weight yarn.

NEEDLES & NOTIONS

1 pair US #10/6mm straight needles
Tapestry needle

GAUGE

14.25 sts = 4"/10cm in pattern stitch, after blocking with ribbing slightly stretched

PATTERN

Cast on 23 sts in pattern.
Follow instructions in "Pattern Basics" on page 20.

SUPER BULKY VERSION

This quick-to-knit weight is perfect for a casual, hip look. A touch of cashmere lends softness and warmth.

FINISHED MEASUREMENTS
4.5" x 41.5"/11.5cm x 105.5cm

YARN
Debbie Bliss Como (90% merino wool, 10% cashmere; 46 yd/42m per 50g ball) (for substitution purposes, 12 sts = 4"/10cm as per ball band); color: #19012, Red; 5 balls.

Or approximately 215 yards of super bulky weight yarn.

NEEDLES & NOTIONS
1 pair US 15/10mm straight needles
Tapestry needle

GAUGE
13 sts = 4"/10cm in pattern stitch, after blocking with ribbing slightly stretched

PATTERN
Cast on 15 sts in pattern.
Follow instructions in "Pattern Basics" on page 20.

CHAPTER 2: SURPRISINGLY SIMPLE STITCHES

Merely by combining knit and purl stitches, an amazing array of looks can emerge. Solid colored yarns lend themselves to sophisticated geometric patterns or flights of frivolity.

On the other hand, we knitters adore the amazing array of colorfully dyed yarns now available. How many times do we come home from the yarn store with a bag full of striped or variegated yarn, but with no idea of what to do with it? Most likely we fell in love with the tantalizing color combinations peeking out from a ball of yarn, or speaking to us from a hank hanging on the wall. Some of the simplest stitch patterns turn these special yarns into wonderful gifts or accessories for our own wardrobe.

EUCLID'S ELEMENTS

Euclid's Elements is a study in positive and negative space using bold geometric forms. The pattern works well in bright colors, adding a lively splash of color to a woman's outfit. Worked in a neutral beige, putty, or grey, the scarf's graphic architectural elements are also well-suited for a man.

FINISHED MEASUREMENTS
6.5" x 80"/16.5cm x 203cm

YARN
Rowan Cashsoft DK (57% extrafine merino wool, 33% acrylic microfibre, 10% cashmere; 142 yd/130m per 50g ball) (for substitution purposes 22 sts/30 rows = 4"/10cm as per ball band); color: #501, Sweet; 5 balls.

Or approximately 540 yards of DK weight yarn.

NEEDLES & NOTIONS
1 pair US #6/4mm straight needles
Tapestry needle

GAUGE
22 sts/30 rows = 4"/10cm in stockinette stitch

PATTERN NOTES
If you're new to using charts, you'll find helpful hints in the Techniques chapter.

If you want a shorter or longer scarf, simply adjust the number of pattern repeats that you work.

This pattern uses a chained selvedge. For all rows, including chart, it is worked as: Sl 1 purlwise wyif, work to last st, k1.

PATTERN
Cast on 38 sts.
Setup rows: Rows 1-6: Sl1 wyif, move yarn to back and knit to end.

Euclid's Elements Pattern
Work rows 1-42 of the chart 16 times or follow written instructions below:
Row 1: Sl1 wyif, k1, p13, k7, p1, k13, p1, k1.
Row 2: Sl1 wyif, k2, p11, k3, p7, k11, p2, k1.
Row 3: Sl1 wyif, k3, p9, k7, p5, k9, p3, k1.
Row 4: Sl1 wyif, k4, p7, k7, p7, k7, p4, k1.
Row 5: Sl1 wyif, k5, p5, k7, p9, k5, p5, k1.
Row 6: Sl1 wyif, k6, p3, k11, p7, k3, p6, k1.

Row 7: Sl1 wyif, k7, p1, k7, p13, k1, p7, k1.
Row 8: Sl1 wyif, p1, k7, p13, k1, p7, k8.
Row 9: Sl1 wyif, p6, k7, p3, k11, p7, k3.
Row 10: Sl1 wyif, p3, k7, p9, k5, p7, k6.
Row 11: Sl1 wyif, p4, k7, p7, k7, p7, k5
Row 12: Sl1 wyif, p5, k7, p5, k9, p7, k4.

Row 13: Sl1 wyif, p2, k7, p11, k3, p7, k7.
Row 14: Sl1 wyif, p7, k7, p1, k13, p7, k2.
Row 15: Sl1 wyif, k7, p1, k13, p7, k1, p7, k1.

Row 16: Sl1 wyif, k6, p3, k7, p11, k3, p6, k1.
Row 17: Sl1 wyif, k5, p5, k9, p7, k5, p5, k1.
Row 18: Sl1 wyif, k4, p7, k7, p7, k7, p4, k1.

Row 19: Sl1 wyif, k3, p9, k5, p7, k9, p3, k1.
Row 20: Sl1 wyif, k2, p11, k7, p3, k11, p2, k1.
Row 21: Sl1 wyif, k1, p13, k1, p7, k13, p1, k1.
Row 22: Sl1 wyif, p1, k13, p1, k7, p13, k2.
Row 23: Sl1 wyif, p2, k11, p7, k3, p11, k3.
Row 24: Sl1 wyif, p3, k9, p5, k7, p9, k4.

Row 25: Sl1 wyif, p4, k7, p7, k7, p7, k5.
Row 26: Sl1 wyif, p5, k5, p9, k7, p5, k6.
Row 27: Sl1 wyif, p6, k3, p7, k11, p3, k7.
Row 28: Sl1 wyif, p7, k1, p13, k7, p1, k8.
Row 29: Sl1 wyif, k7, p7, k1, p13, k7, p1, k1.
Row 30: Sl1 wyif, k2, p7, k11, p3, k7, p6, k1.

Row 31: Sl1 wyif, k5, p7, k5, p9, k7, p3, k1.
Row 32: Sl1 wyif, k4, p7, k7, p7, k7, p4, k1.
Row 33: Sl1 wyif, k3, p7, k9, p5, k7, p5, k1.

Row 34: Sl1 wyif, k6, p7, k3, p11, k7, p2, k1.
Row 35: Sl1 wyif, k1, p7, k13, p1, k7, p7, k1.
Row 36: Sl1 wyif, p7, k1, p7, k13, p1, k8.

Row 37: Sl1 wyif, p6, k3, p11, k7, p3, k7.
Row 38: Sl1 wyif, p5, k5, p7, k9, p5, k6.
Row 39: Sl1 wyif, p4, k7, p7, k7, p7, k5.
Row 40: Sl1 wyif, p3, k9, p7, k5, p9, k4.
Row 41: Sl1 wyif, p2, k11, p3, k7, p11, k3.
Row 42: Sl1 wyif, p1, k13, p7, k1, p13, k2.

Rep rows 1-42 sixteen times total.

Ending rows:
Rows 1-6: Sl1 wyif, yb knit to end.
Bind off.

FINISHING

Weave in ends. Block without overly stretching out the stitches; the idea is to retain the textural quality.

KEY TO CHART

	Edge Slip St
V	Side 1: Slp wyif
	Side 2: Slp wyif

	knit
☐	Side 1: knit stitch
	Side 2: purl stitch

	purl
●	Side 1: purl stitch
	Side 2: knit stitch

IMITATION LATTICE

All-over stitch patterns offer subtle sophistication. A bamboo blend yarn is a great choice for this scarf due to its beautiful drape; a slight sheen helps define the stitch pattern. This is a very wide scarf, but with a 2"/5cm pattern repeat, you can easily make it the width you want.

FINISHED MEASUREMENTS
9" x 48"/23cm x 122cm

YARN
Sirdar Snuggly Baby Bamboo DK (80% bamboo, 20% wool; 104 yd/95m per 50g ball) (for substitution purposes, 22 sts/28 rows = 4"/10cm as per ball band); color: #159, Jack in a Box; 5 balls.

Or approximately 375 yards of DK weight yarn.

NEEDLES & NOTIONS
1 pair US #6/4mm straight needles
Tapestry needle

GAUGE
22 sts/28 rows = 4"/10cm in stockinette stitch, after blocking

PATTERN NOTE
Pattern stitch is a multiple of 12 sts + 5.

PATTERN
Using a long-tail knit/purl cast-on in pattern (see the Techniques chapter for instructions), cast on 53 sts as follows: K2, p5, (k3, p9) 3 times, k3, p5, k2.

Beginning Section:
Row 1: K7, p3, * k9, p3; rep from * to last 7 sts, k7.
Row 2: K2, p5, * k3, p9; rep from * to last 10 sts, k3, p5, k2.
Rep these 2 rows until piece measures approx 3"/7.5cm, ending with row 2.

Middle Section:
Row 1: K6, * p5, k7; rep from * to last 11 sts, p5, k6.
Row 2 and all even numbered rows: K2, then knit all knit sts and purl all purl sts to last 2 sts, k2.
Row 3: K5, * p3, k1, p3, k5; rep from * to end.
Row 5: K4, * p3, k3; rep from * to last st, k1.
Row 7: K3, * p3, k5, p3, k1; rep from * to last 2 sts, k2.
Row 9: K2, p3, * k7, p5; rep from * to last 12 sts, k7, p3, k2.
Row 11: K2, p2, * k9, p3; rep from * to last 13 sts, k9, p2, k2.

Row 13: K2, p3, * k7, p5; rep from * to last 12 sts, k7, p3, k2.
Row 15: K3, * p3, k5, p3, k1; rep from * to last 2 sts, k2.
Row 17: K4, * p3, k3; rep from * to last st, k1.
Row 19: K5, * p3, k1, p3, k5; rep from * to end.
Row 21: K6, * p5, k7; rep from * to last 11 sts, p5, k6.
Row 23: K7, * p3, k9; rep from * to last 10 sts, p3, k7.
Rep rows 1-24 until scarf measures 45"/114.5cm, or 3"/7.5cm less than desired length, ending with row 24.

Ending Section:
Row 1: K7, * p3, k9; rep from * to last 10 sts, p3, k7.
Row 2: K2, p5, k3, * p9, k3; rep from * to last 7 sts, p5, k2.
Rep these 2 rows until piece measures approx 48"/122cm, ending with row 1.

Bind off in pattern.

FINISHING
Weave in ends. Block.

IMITATION LATTICE CHART

As seen from side 1

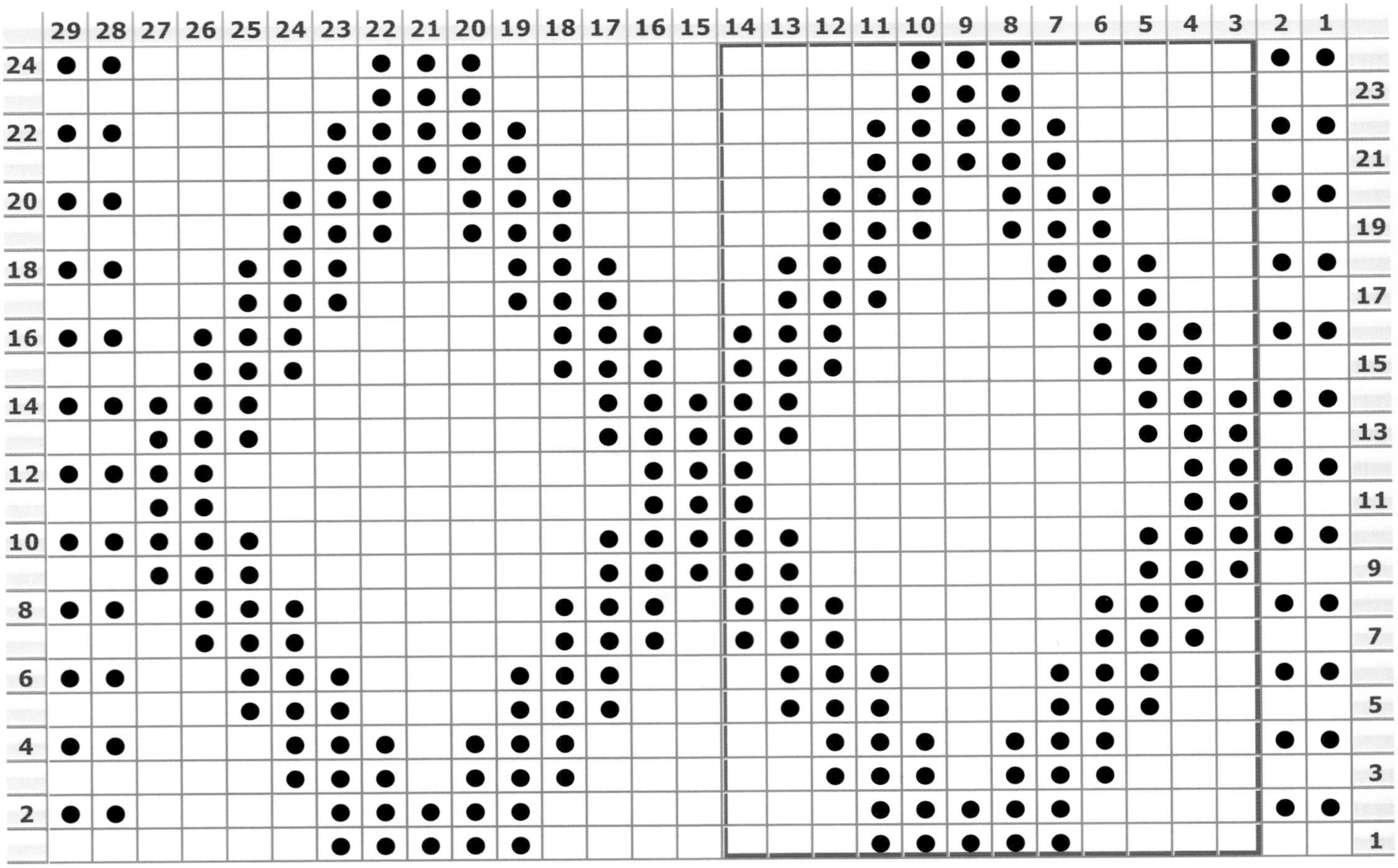

| | 29 | 28 | 27 | 26 | 25 | 24 | 23 | 22 | 21 | 20 | 19 | 18 | 17 | 16 | 15 | 14 | 13 | 12 | 11 | 10 | 9 | 8 | 7 | 6 | 5 | 4 | 3 | 2 | 1 | |

KEY TO CHART

☐ Knit on side 1; purl on side 2

● Purl on side 1; knit on side 2

34

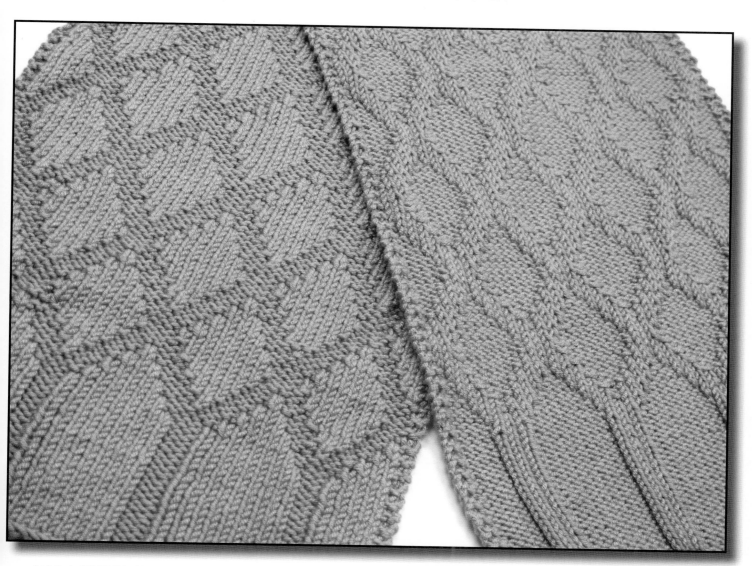

SIDE 1 SHOWN AT LEFT
SIDE 2 SHOWN AT RIGHT

LINEN STITCH TO THE RESCUE

I adore the richness of hand-dyed, semi-solid yarn, the vibrant colors of variegated yarn, and the intriguing textures in thick-thin yarn. But sometimes I don't know what to do with them.

The linen stitch lets me transform these yarns into entirely different looks. I use linen stitch when I want to soften the stripey effects of semi-solids, lend a painterly appearance to variegateds, or turn a thick-thin yarn into a fabric filled with intriguing texture. The stitch's versatility makes it a great tool to have in your knitterly toolbox.

BASIC LINEN STITCH PATTERN

Because the linen stitch causes the knitted fabric to pull inward, it's typically worked on needles one or two sizes larger than the ball band calls for. You may need to cast on and bind off more firmly than usual to avoid flaring at the top and bottom of the scarf. Use the gauges suggested below to create a linen stitch scarf of your own. Here's how you do it:

Using an even number of stitches, cast on the amount that will give you the width you want. You can refer to the suggested gauges shown below as a guideline.

Slip all stitches purlwise.

Linen stitch:
Row 1: * K1, sl1 wyif; rep from * to end. (Be sure to end with the yarn in the front of the work).
Row 2: * P1, sl1 wyib; rep from * to end. (End with yarn in the back of the work).
Rep these 2 rows until you like the length of your scarf, then bind off firmly and weave in the ends.

You can use the examples below as a springboard to make your own creation. Want the scarf wider or narrower? Just adjust the number of cast-on stitches (keeping them an even number). Want it longer? A little advance planning will ensure that you buy enough yarn for your project.

SEMI-SOLIDS

Tone-on-tone yarns can produce a stripy effect, which the linen stitch does wonders to mute. (See photo at left.)

FINISHED MEASUREMENTS
5.75" x 56"/14.5cm x 142cm

YARN
Madelinetosh Tosh DK (100% superwash merino wool; 225 yd/206m per 105g skein) (for substitution purposes, 20-22 sts = 4"/10cm as per ball band); color: Terra; 2 skeins.

Or approximately 295 yards of DK weight yarn.

NEEDLES & NOTIONS
1 pair US#6/4mm straight needles
Tapestry needle

GAUGE
26.5 sts = 4"/10cm in Linen stitch

PATTERN
Cast on 38 sts.

Work in Linen stitch until scarf measures 56"/142cm or desired length.

Bind off and weave in ends.

VARIEGATED

Variegated yarns take on a painterly, almost impressionist or pointillist look. The resulting pattern can be an unexpected delight! I like to use yarns with at least four colors for smaller areas of pooling.

The yarn you use and the width you choose will produce a pattern that could be quite similar or different from the one shown here. How the yarn is dyed, the number of colors and their length on the fiber, all conspire for a unique effect. For me, that's half the fun of making this scarf!

FINISHED MEASUREMENTS
5.25" x 72"/13.5cm x 183cm

YARN
Lorna's Laces Shepherd Worsted (100% superwash wool; 225 yd/206m per 4 oz skein) (for substitution purposes, 18 sts = 4"/10cm as per ball band); color: #105 Glenwood; 2 skeins.

Or approximately 340 yards of worsted weight yarn.

NEEDLES & NOTIONS
1 pair US #9/5.5mm straight needles
Tapestry needle

GAUGE
23 sts = 4"/10cm in Linen stitch

PATTERN
Cast on 30 sts.

Work in Linen stitch until scarf measures 72"/183cm or desired length.

Bind off and weave in ends.

TEXTURE

Sometimes I'm in the mood for lots of texture. Thick-thin yarns create an intriguing mixture of smooth and bumpy surfaces, with seemingly capricious color placement.

This super bulky yarn was worked up on big, chunky needles for a fast, gratifying knit.

FINISHED MEASUREMENTS

5.25" x 60"/13.5cm x 152.5cm

YARN

Plymouth Yarn Expression (55% wool, 45% acrylic microfiber, 55 yd/50m per 50g ball) (for substitution purposes, 10 sts = 4"/10cm as per ball band); color: #3696; 3 balls.

Or approximately 140 yards of super bulky yarn.

NEEDLES & NOTIONS

1 pair US #17/12.75mm straight needles
Tapestry needle

GAUGE

12 sts = 4"/10cm in Linen stitch

PATTERN

Cast on 16 sts.

Work in Linen stitch until scarf measures 60"/152.5cm or desired length.

Bind off and weave in ends.

MARVELOUS MOSS

Moss stitch is very versatile, looking attractive in solids as well as multi-colored yarns. It's a great choice for men's scarves, since the texture is interesting without being too busy.

FINISHED MEASUREMENTS
7" x 77"/18cm x 195.5cm

YARN
Rowan Colourscape Chunky (100% lambswool, 175 yd/160m per 100g ball) (for substitution purposes, 14 sts/18 rows = 4"/10cm as per ball band); color: #438, Autumn; 2 balls.

Or approximately 280 yards of chunky weight yarn.

NEEDLES & NOTIONS
1 pair US #10.5/6.5mm straight needles
Tapestry needle

GAUGE
14.5 sts = 4"/10cm in moss stitch

PATTERN NOTES
When using a yarn with a long stripe sequence or shaded stripes, you may want to match the colors when you finish with one ball of yarn and start the next. When you get to within several yards of the end of the first ball, stop. Pull a few yards out of the second ball of yarn. See where the colors match; end the first ball and start the second where the colors match.

Moss stitch is a multiple of 2 sts + 1.

PATTERN
Cast on 27 sts.

Row 1: K1, * p1, k1; rep from * to end.
Row 2: K1, * p1, k1; rep from * to end.
Row 3: P1, * k1, p1; rep from * to end.
Row 4: P1, * k1, p1; rep from * to end.

Rep rows 1-4 until scarf measures 77"/195.5cm or desired length.

Bind off.

FINISHING
Weave in ends. Block.

MIXER

A variety of simple knit/purl stitch patterns make up this scarf. Knit this pattern as is, or use it as inspiration to create your own combination of stitch patterns.

FINISHED MEASUREMENTS
7.5" x 68"/19cm x 172.5cm

YARN
Cascade 220 Wool (100% Peruvian highland wool; 220 yd/201m per 100g skein) (for substitution purposes, 18-20 sts = 4"/10cm as per ball band); color: #8910, Citron; 2 skeins.

Or approximately 420 yards of worsted weight yarn.

NEEDLES & NOTIONS
1 pair US #7/4.5 mm straight needles
1 pair US #8/5mm straight needles
Tapestry needle

GAUGE
19 sts/27rows = 4"/10cm in stockinette stitch on smaller needles, after blocking

PATTERN NOTE
If you want to alter the length of your scarf, one pattern sequence measures about 8"/20.5cm.

SPECIAL ABBREVIATIONS AND TERMS
M1 = Make one purlwise by inserting the left-hand needle under the bar between the stitches from back to front. Purl this strand through the front.

S2KP2 (sl2, k1, p2sso)= Centered Double Decrease (WS): slip 2 sts together as if to knit, knit one, pass both slipped sts over the knitted st.

PATTERN
With larger needles, loosely cast on 33 sts.

Beginning Section:
Work either Chart A (a total of 2 repeats) or written instructions as follows:
Row 1 (RS): * K1, yo, [k1, p1] 7 times, k1, yo; rep from * to last st, k1. [37 sts]
Row 2: * K1, p2, [k1, p1] 7 times, p1; rep from * to last st, k1.

Row 3: * K2, yo, [k1, p1] 7 times, k1, yo, k1; rep from * to last st, k1. [41 sts]
Row 4: * K2, p2, [k1, p1] 7 times, p1, k1; rep from * to last st, k1.
Row 5: * K3, yo, [k1, p1] 7 times, k1, yo, k2; rep from * to last st, k1. [45 sts]
Row 6: * K3, p2, [k1, p1] 7 times, p1, k2; rep from * to last st, k1.
Row 7: * K4, yo, [k1, p1] 7 times, k1, yo, k3; rep from * to last st, k1. [49 sts]
Row 8: * K4, p2, [k1, p1] 7 times, p1, k3; rep from * to last st, k1.
Row 9: * K5, [ssk] 4 times, k1, [k2tog] 3 times, k4; rep from * to last st, k1. [35 sts]

With smaller needles, knit 1 row.
Next row (RS): Knit 17, m1, k18. [36 sts]
Knit 1 row.

PATTERN SEQUENCE:
Work Chart B, or instructions as follow, 8 times:

First Seed Stitch Section:
Row 1 (RS): * K1, p1; rep from * to end.
Row 2: * P1, k1; rep from * to end.
Rows 3-7: Rep rows 1 & 2, ending with row 1.
Rows 8-10: Knit.

Dropped Stitch Section:
Row 11 (RS): Knit, wrapping yarn around needle twice for each st instead of the usual once.
Row 12: Knit, dropping extra wrap from each st.
Rows 13-15: Knit.

Triangle Section:
Row 16 (WS): * P1, k5; rep from * to end.
Row 17: * P4, k2; rep from * to end.
Row 18: * P3, k3; rep from * to end.
Row 19: * P2, k4; rep from * to end.
Row 20: * P5, k1; rep from * to end.
Rows 21-23: Knit.

Dropped Stitch Section:
Row 24 (WS): Knit, wrapping yarn around needle twice for each st instead of the usual once.
Row 25: Knit, dropping extra wrap from each st.
Rows 26-28: Knit.

Second Seed Stitch Section:
Row 29 (RS): * P1, k1; rep from * to end.
Row 30: * K1, p1; rep from * to end.
Rows 31-32: Rep rows 29 & 30.
Rows 33-36: Knit.

Wave Section:
Row 37 (RS): P2, * p3, k3, p4, k3, p3; rep from * to last 2 sts, p2.
Row 38: K2, * k2, p3, k6, p3, k2; rep from * to last 2 sts, k2.
Row 39: K2, * k4, p8, k4; rep from * to last 2 sts, k2.
Row 40: P2, * p3, k3, p4, k3, p3; rep from * to last 2 sts, p2.
Row 41: K2, * k2, p3, k6, p3, k2; rep from * to last 2 sts, k2.
Row 42: K2, * k4, p8, k4; rep from * to last 2 sts, k2.
Rows 43-48: Rep rows 37-42.
Rows 49-51: Knit.

Dropped Stitch section
Row 52 (WS): Knit, wrapping yarn around needle twice for each st instead of the usual once.
Row 53: Knit, dropping extra wrap from each st.
Rows 54-56: Knit.

Repeat entire Pattern Sequence (from First Seed Stitch to final Dropped Stitch sections) 7 more times. Scarf measures approx 64.5"/164cm, or about 3.25"/8.5cm less than desired length.

Ending Section:
Last Seed Stitch Section:
Row 1 (RS): * K1, p1; rep from * to end.
Row 2: * P1, k1; rep from * to end.
Rows 3-7: Rep rows 1 & 2, ending with row 1.
Rows 8-9: Knit.

Next row (WS): K17, k2tog, k17. [35 sts]
Knit 1 row.

With larger needles, work Chart C, or written instructions as follows:
Row 1: * K6, [m1, k1] 7 times, k4; rep from * to last st, k1. [49 sts]
Row 2: * K4, p2, [k1, p1] 7 times, p1, k3; rep from * to last st, k1.
Row 3: * K4, yo, k2tog, p1, [k1, p1] 6 times, ssk, yo, k3; rep from * to last st, k1.
Row 4: * K2, k2tog , p2, [k1, p1] 7 times, p1, ssk, k1; rep from * to last st, k1. [45 sts]
Row 5: * K3, yo, k2tog, p1, [k1, p1] 6 times, ssk, yo, k2; rep from * to last st, k1.
Row 6: * K1, k2tog, p2, [k1, p1] 7 times, p1, ssk; rep from * to last st, k1. [41 sts]
Row 7: * K2, yo, k2tog, p1, [k1, p1] 6 times, ssk, yo, k1; rep from * to last st, k1.
Row 8: K2tog, p2, [k1, p1] 7 times, p1, S2KP2, p2, [k1, p1] 7 times, p1, ssk. [37 sts]
Row 9: * K1, yo, k2tog, p1, [k1, p1] 6 times, ssk, yo; rep from * to last st, k1.

Bind off very loosely in pattern as follows: * 3 purlwise, [knitwise, purlwise] 7 times, purlwise; rep from * to last st, purlwise.

FINISHING
Weave in ends. Block scarf, pinning ends to shape fans along scarf edge.

MAKE IT YOUR OWN

You can find lots of reversible knit/purl stitch patterns in stitch dictionaries. Or you can make up your own, as I did for the "Waves" Section in the Mixer scarf.

Add increases or decreases as necessary in the garter rows to make the stitch count work out for your pattern.

CHART A

25	24	23	22	21	20	19	18	17	16	15	14	13	12	11	10	9	8	7	6	5	4	3	2	1

Rows (left side): 8, 6, 4, 2 — Rows (right side): 9, 7, 5, 3, 1

KEY TO CHART A

▨ (grey)	**No Stitch**	
☐	**knit**	Knit on RS, purl on WS
⊙	**yo**	Yarn over
●	**purl**	Purl on RS, knit on WS
◺	**ssk**	Slip one stitch as if to knit, Slip another stitch as if to knit. Insert left-hand needle into front of these 2 stitches and knit them together
◹	**k2tog**	Knit two stitches together as one stitch

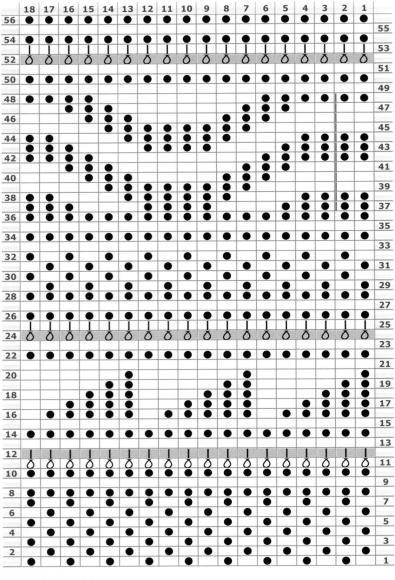

Note: for lines 37-48 of Chart B (the Wave Section), refer to the line-by-line written instructions.

KEY TO CHART B

☐ **knit**
Knit on RS, purl on WS

● **purl**
Purl on RS, knit on WS

⚯ **K1 elongated RS**
Knit one stitch wrappng yarn twice. (Extra wap will be dropped on next row)

| **Knit Dropping Wrap WS**
Knit, dropping extra wrap

⚯ **K1 elongated WS**
Knit one stitch wrapping yarn twice. (Extra wrap will be dropped on next row)

| **Knit Dropping Wrap RS**
Knit, dropping extra wrap

KEY TO CHART C

☐ **knit**
Knit on RS, purl on WS

M **Make 1 Purlwise**
Insert left needle from back to front under ladder. Purl this strand through the front

● **purl**
Purl on RS, knit on RS

○ **yo**
Yarn over

╱ **k2tog**
Knit two stitches together as one stitch

╱ **ssk**
Slip one stitch as if to knit. Slip another stitch as if to knit. Insert left-hand needle into front of these 2 stitches and knit them together

▨ **No Stitch**

╱ **Ssk on WS**
Ssk on WS

╱ **K2tog on WS**
K2tog on WS

⋀ **S2KP2 on WS**
Slip 2 sts tog as if to k2tog, knit 1, pass both sl sts over the knitted stitch

SEEDED STRIPES

The easiest way to get stripes into a scarf is to let the yarn do it for you. Self-striping yarn can be fun to work with, as the color changes keep the knitting interesting.

The super-simple seed stitch adds texture to this striped scarf.

FINISHED MEASUREMENTS
5" x 74"/12.5cm x 188cm

YARN
Elegant Yarns Kaleidoscope (100% wool; 174 yd/160m per 100g ball) (for substitution purposes 5.5 sts = 1"/2.5cm as per ball band); color: CK03; 2 balls.

Or approximately 265 yards of DK weight yarn

NEEDLES & NOTIONS
1 pair US #6/4mm straight needles
Tapestry needle

GAUGE
20 sts = 4"/10cm in pattern stitch, after blocking

PATTERN NOTE
When getting close to running out of one ball and starting a new one, plan ahead to keep the colors consistent. You may need to pull out several yards of the new ball to get to the color that matches the color you left off on the previous ball.

PATTERN
Loosely cast on 24 sts.

Row 1: * K1, p1; rep from * to end.
Row 2: * P1, k1; rep from * to end.

Rep these 2 rows until scarf measures 74"/188cm or desired length.

Bind off loosely.

FINISHING
Weave in ends. Block scarf.

SHORT AND SWEET

In this short scarf, one end pulls through the other to form a sweet accent. Easy to make, this is the perfect pattern for gift giving. And since it uses just one skein, this project makes great use of that special hand-dyed yarn that's been hibernating in your stash.

FINISHED MEASUREMENTS
4.5" x 30"/11.5cm x 76cm

YARN
Madelinetosh Tosh DK (100% superwash merino wool; 225 yd/206m per 105g skein) (for substitution purposes, 20-22 sts = 4"/10cm as per ball band); color: Nostalgia; 1 skein.

Or approximately 100 yards of DK weight yarn

NEEDLES & NOTIONS
1 pair US #6/4mm straight needles
1 set US #6/4mm dpns
Tapestry needle

GAUGE
23 sts/30 rows = 4"/10cm in Moss stitch, after blocking, or
22 sts/28 rows = 4"/10cm in stockinette stitch, after blocking

PATTERN NOTES
This scarf consists of five segments: a beginning, a slot to pull the scarf through, the neck, a narrow section that rests inside the slot, and the ending section.

You can alter the fit by trying on the scarf as you go. By working a shorter or longer neck section before starting the narrowed segment, you can achieve a tighter or looser fit.

Moss stitch is a multiple of 2 sts + 1.

PATTERN
Cast on 3 sts.
Beginning Section:
Row 1 (RS): Kfb twice, k1. [5 sts]
Row 2: P1, * k1, p1; rep from * to end.
Row 3: Kfb, k1, p1, kfb, k1. [7 sts]
Row 4: P1, * k1, p1; rep from * to end.
Row 5: Kfb, * k1, p1; rep from * to last 2 sts, kfb, k1. [2 sts increased]
Rep rows 4 and 5 until 25 sts are on the needle.
Rep row 4 once more.

Slot:
Divide sts: Using 2 dpns (dpn1 and dpn2), and holding dpn1 in

front of work, * sl1 knit st onto dpn1, sl1 purl st onto dpn2; rep from * to last st, sl1 onto dpn1. [13 sts on dpn1, 12 sts on dpn2]
On dpn1, slide sts to end of needle where working yarn is.

Row 1: Using spare dpn, knit sts on dpn1.
Row 2: Purl.
Rep rows 1 and 2 another 8 times for a total of 18 rows of stockinette stitch. Break yarn.
On dpn2, join yarn and work 18 rows stockinette as on dpn1 above.
Restore sts to single straight needle as follows: With stockinette side facing, sl1 from dpn1 to straight needle, * sl1 from dpn2, sl1 from dpn1; rep from * to end. [25 sts]

Neck Section: If you want a tighter fit, make this section shorter, for a looser fit make it longer.
Row 1: P1, * k1, p1; rep from * to end.
Row 2: K1, * p1, k1; rep from * to end.
Row 3: K1, * p1, k1; rep from * to end.
Row 4: P1, * k1, p1; rep from * to end.
Rep rows 1-4 until piece measures 17"/43cm from slot, or desired length, ending with row 4.

Narrow Section:
Note: Work slipped sts firmly to draw sts inward.
Row 1 (RS): K1, * sl1 wyif, k1; rep from * to end.
Row 2: Sl1 wyif, * k1, sl1 wyif; rep from * to end.
Rep rows 1 and 2 another 7 times for a total of 16 rows.

Ending Section:
Row 1 (RS): K1, * p1, k1; rep from * to end.
Row 2: P1, * k1, p1; rep from * to end.
Row 3: P1, * k1, p1; rep from * to end.
Row 4: K1, * p1, k1; rep from * to end.
Rep rows 1-4 twice more for a total of 12 rows.

Decrease Section:
Row 1 (RS): P2tog, * k1, p1; rep from * to last 3 sts, k1, p2tog.
Row 2: K1, * p1, k1; rep from * to end.
Rep rows 1 and 2 until 5 sts remain.
Rep row 1 once more.
Bind off.

FINISHING
Weave in ends. Block scarf, shaping end sections as desired. I like to use flexible wires to give the end sections slightly rounded sides.

TUX

Remember the ruffled tuxedo shirts that were popular in the '70s? This scarf evokes that retro look. Worked lengthwise, the ruffles are formed by simple decreases and increases. This is designed to be long and worn wrapped many times around the neck. Ruffles are especially pretty and feminine!

FINISHED MEASUREMENTS
3" x 82"/7.5cm x 208.5cm

YARN
Berroco Ultra Alpaca Light (50% superfine alpaca, 50% Peruvian wool; 144 yd/133m per 50g skein) (for substitution purposes, 23 sts/32 rows = 4"/10cm as per ball band); color: #4201, Winter White; 5 skeins.

Or approximately 540 yards of dk weight yarn

NEEDLES & NOTIONS
1 US #5/3.75mm circular needle, 60"/150cm or longer, lace points recommended
Lots and lots of stitch markers
Tapestry needle

GAUGE
23 sts/32 rows = 4"/10cm in stockinette stitch, after blocking

PATTERN NOTES
Cast-on yardage: When you get ready to work a gauge swatch, it's the perfect time to estimate the yardage you'll need to cast on. With so many stitches to cast on, you wouldn't want to get caught short! Refer to the Techniques chapter, page 12, for ideas about estimating the yardage you'll need for the long-tail cast-on.

In order to prevent curling, the cast-on and bind-off instructions call for purling the knits and knitting the purls.

Sometimes I like a really long scarf like this, to wrap around my neck a couple of times. While it requires a LOT of stitches to be cast on, the scarf is easy to knit and the effect is worth the effort. That said, if you'd like to make the scarf shorter, estimate about 1.75"/4.5cm per repeat.

The cast-on instructions call for markers to be placed every 26 sts to separate each repeat of the pattern. This will help you to maintain your sanity both when counting the cast-on stitches and keeping your place as you establish the stitch pattern.

Pattern stitch is a multiple of 26 sts, plus 14 extra sts for the half-ruffles at the beginning and end.

SPECIAL ABBREVIATIONS
M1K: Make one knitwise by inserting the left-hand needle under the bar between the sts from front to back. Knit through the back loop.

M1P: Make one purlwise by inserting the left-hand needle under the bar between the sts from back to front. Purl through the front loop.

Kfbf: Knit into the front, back, and then front of the stitch.

Pfbf: Purl into the front, back, and then front of the stitch.

PATTERN
Using a long-tail knit/purl cast-on (see the Techniques chapter for instructions), loosely cast on 1,210 sts as follows: P7, PM, [k13, p13, PM] 46 times, k7.

Rows 1-8: K7, * p13, k13; rep from * to last 7 sts, p7.
Row 9 (dec row): [K2tog] 3 times, k1, * [p2tog] 6 times, p1, [k2tog] 6 times, k1; rep from * to last 7 sts, p1, [p2tog] 3 times. [14 sts in each section and 4 sts at each end (652 sts total)]
Row 10: K4, * p7, k7; rep from * to last 4 sts, p4.
Row 11 (dec row): K3tog, k1, * [p3tog] 2 times, p1, [k3tog] twice, k1; rep from * to last 4 sts, p1, p3tog. [6 sts in each section and 2 sts at each end (280 sts total)]

Rows 12-14: Knit.
Row 15 (inc row): Kfbf, k1, * [pfbf] twice, p1, [kfbf] twice, k1; rep from * to last 2 sts, p1, pfbf. [14 sts in each section and 4 sts at each end (652 sts total)]
Row 16: K4, * p7, k7; rep from * to last 4 sts, p4.
Row 17 (inc row): [K1, m1k] 3 times, k1, * [p1, m1p] 6 times, p1, [k1, m1k] 6 times, k1; rep from * to last 4 sts, [p1, m1p] 3 times, p1. [26 sts in each section and 7 sts at each end (1,210 sts total)]

Note: After Row 18, you don't really need the stitch markers; you can remove them as you come to them, or leave them in if you find they're helpful.

Rows 18-25: K7, * p13, k13; rep from * to last 7 sts, p7.

To reduce curling, loosely bind off the purl sts knitwise and the knit sts purlwise.

FINISHING

Weave in ends.

Wet block by laying out the scarf, shaping the ruffles by hand, first on one side, then gently turning the scarf over and shaping the ruffles on the other side. (Do not pin.)

MAKE IT YOUR OWN

Many knit/purl combinations – such as the examples shown on this page – produce wonderful reversible designs. It can be a lot of fun to look through stitch dictionaries hunting for ones that appeal to you. Some reversible patterns will look the same on both sides, such as the seed or moss stitch. Others, like the Imitation Lattice, will look different – but appealing – on either side.

To come up with creations of your own, I suggest grabbing a pencil and some graph paper. Play with combinations of knits and purls to make your own stitch patterns. Even better than conventional graph paper is specialty paper in which the squares are proportioned to the stitch size.

See the Resources section at the end of the book for places to download proportional graph paper.

ZIGZAG

I learned this multidirectional knitting technique from JC Briar, and used it to create a herringbone effect. You have a choice of scarf ends: either pointed (if you're up for a bit of a challenge) or square.

FINISHED MEASUREMENTS
4.75" x 82"/12cm x 208.5cm

YARN
Wisdom Yarns Poems (100% wool; 109 yd/100m per 50g ball) (for substitution purposes, 16-20 sts = 4"/10cm as per ball band); color: #589 Tokyo (Pointed Ends version) or #590 Sakura (Square Ends version); 4 balls.

Note: Yardage includes extra for transitioning colors at joins. For Pointed Ends version, approximately 360 yards of worsted weight yarn; for Square Ends version, approximately 410 yards of worsted weight yarn

NEEDLES & NOTIONS
2 pairs #7/4.5mm straight needles (only 1 pair needed for Square Ends version)
Locking stitch markers
Tapestry needle

GAUGE
18 sts/38 rows = 4"/10cm in garter stitch, after blocking

PATTERN NOTES
The only unusual part of this pattern is that you will be turning your work midway through knitting a row. Just remember that on most rows, once you k2tog, you'll turn the work over, slip the k2tog stitch you just formed, then knit to the end of the row. Simple, really!

Because you're forming partial instead of full rows, and then turning the work, the instructions refer to "Steps" rather than "Rows."

For the first bit of knitting, it may seem like the pattern isn't working out at all like the photo shows. After a few repeats, the pattern will become apparent, and you can breathe easy!

Joining new balls of yarn: To make a smooth visual transition to a new ball, pull yarn out of the new ball until you find a color that looks like a natural transition from the old color. They don't need to be exact, just subtle.

SPECIAL ABBREVIATIONS AND TERMS
RM: Remove marker

Gap: Space between k2tog and next st on needle

Dormant sts: Sts on your left-hand needle that have not been knitted

POINTED ENDS VERSION

Pointy Beginning Hint: In the beginning when making the triangles, attach a removable marker to the RS of fabric to make it easier to keep track of which side is facing you. That way, when the marker is facing you, you'll know to start your row with an increase. You can remove the marker once the triangle's shape becomes obvious.

First Triangle:
Cast on 1 st.
Row 1 (RS): Kfb. [2 sts]
Row 2 (WS): Knit. Attach locking marker to RS of work.
Row 3 (RS): Kfb, k to end. [3 sts]
Rep rows 2 and 3 until you have 20 sts, or desired number (this needs to be divisible by 2).
Break yarn, keeping the work on the needle.
PM after 10th st (or at point halfway between total number of sts).
Set aside while you make the second triangle.

Second Triangle:
Cast on 1 st.
Row 1 (RS): Kfb. [2 sts]
Row 2 (WS): Knit. Attach locking marker to RS of work.
Row 3 (RS): Kfb, k to end. [3 sts]
Row 4 (WS): Knit.
Rep rows 3 and 4 until you have 10 sts, or half the number of sts you ended with for the first triangle.

Join Triangles:
On second triangle, kfb, k to last st, sl last st onto right-hand needle, then sl this st onto the first triangle's needle; you will see that the RS of the second triangle faces you, while the WS of the first triangle faces you. K2tog to join last st from second triangle to first st of first triangle. You'll see

there is a gap between the k2tog and the next st on the needle. Turn work.
Next row (new RS): Sl1 (you're slipping the k2tog), k to end. [30 sts] You can now RM from the triangle points.

Zigzag Pattern:
Step 1: Kfb, k to last st before gap, k2tog. Turn.
Step 2: Sl1 wyif, k to end. [30 sts]
Step 3: Rep steps 1 and 2 until your k2tog brings you to your marker; leaving marker in place, knit across the 10 "dormant" sts.
Step 4: Kfb, k to last st before marker, RM, k2tog; move marker to 10 sts in from far end of left-hand needle. Turn. [30 sts]
Step 5: Sl1, k to end.
Rep Steps 1-5 for pattern until scarf reaches desired length.

Pointed End:
Rep Steps 1 and 2 of pattern until your k2tog brings you to 1 st before marker, ending with step 2.
Next step: Bind off to 2 sts before marker, k2tog, bind off 1 st, RM, ssk, bind off rem sts.

FINISHING

Weave in ends. I find that weaving in the cast-on tails along the inside edges of the triangles (from points to join), helps the ends to hold their shape. Block.

SQUARE ENDS VERSION

Squared Beginning:
Cast on 1 st.
Row 1: Kfb. [2 sts]
Increase Row: Kfb, k to end. [3 sts]
Rep increase row until you have 30 sts on your needle. (If you're designing your own, rep this row until either of the short edges of your work is the width you want your scarf to be. Remember that the number of stitches on your needle needs to be divisible by 3.)
PM 10 sts (or 1/3 of the total) in from far end of needle.

Setup rows:
Row 1: K2. Turn.
Row 2: Sl1, k to end of row. You will see there is a gap where you turned your work and slipped the stitch.
Row 3: Kfb, k2tog. Turn.
Row 4: Sl1, k to end.

Zigzag Pattern (same as in Pointed Ends version):
Step 1 (WS): Kfb, k to last st before gap, k2tog. Turn.
Step 2: Sl1, k to end.
Step 3: Rep steps 1 and 2 until your k2tog brings you to your marker; leaving marker in place, knit across the 10 "dormant" sts.
Step 4: Kfb, k to last st before marker, RM, k2tog; move marker to 10 sts in from far end of left-hand needle. Turn.
Step 5: Sl1, k to end.
Rep steps 1-5 for pattern until scarf measures approx 82"/208.5cm or desired length.

Squared Ending:
Continue in pattern until you have 15 sts on your right-hand needle after step 1's k2tog. (If designing your own, this will be half the total sts, or half + 1 if your total is an odd number). Turn as before, sl1 and knit to end. RM.
Step 1: K to last st before gap, k2tog. Turn.
Step 2: Sl1, k to last 2 sts, k2tog.
Rep steps 1 and 2 until 3 sts remain. (On last step 2, instead of the final k2tog, there may only be 1 st, in which case just knit it.)
Next step: K1, k2tog. Do not turn.

Binding off: Pass 2nd st on right-hand needle over first st, as for binding off.

FINISHING
Weave in ends. Block.

MAKE IT YOUR OWN

Would you like to use yarn with a different gauge, or maybe make your scarf a different width? How do you figure out the number of stitches you need to end up with on your needle? First, you need to know your gauge, so you can plug the stitches per inch into the formula. Then dust off your geometry and the Pythagorean Theorem, which applies to right triangles. It's easier than it sounds!

You may remember the theorem as $A^2 + B^2 = C^2$, but when, as in this case, the angles on your triangle are 45°, 45° and 90°, you can use an even simpler formula:

B x {number of stitches per inch} x 1.4 = C

... where B = the desired width, C = the number of stitches you want to end up with, and 1.4 is a close

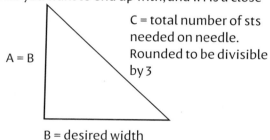

C = total number of sts needed on needle. Rounded to be divisible by 3

A = B

B = desired width

enough equivalent to the √2.

As an example, let's say your gauge is 4 sts/inch. First, decide on the width you want the scarf to be. Suppose you want it to be 5" across. The width across the scarf is represented by B, or 5". Now you need to use this number (5"), to figure out the length of the hypotenuse, or C.
C represents the stitches that are on your needle after you've made the desired number of increases.

B x {number of stitches per inch} x 1.4 = C
5 x {4 sts per inch} x 1.4 = 28 sts

However, the total on your needle needs to be divisible by 3, so you'll use the closest number that will work – in this case, 27.

You are now free to come up with whatever width scarf you desire, using whatever gauge of yarn you want. Have fun!

CHAPTER 3: MULTI-YARN MARVELS

Combining different yarns in a variety of ways opens up whole new worlds of color and texture. One day I'm in the mood to accent my favorite variegated yarn with a contrasting solid, the next day I want to throw lots of solids together for a completely different look. Starting with just a few multi-yarn patterns, I can play with an endless array of possibilities.

I used to think that a striped scarf had to have a wrong side, with all the little purl bumps forming an obvious join at the color change. Think again! Here I offer up stripes several different ways – using a composite yarn (or a whole bunch of yarns from your stash), using shading to blend from one color to another, and applying reversible techniques to bold stripes. Let your imagination soar as you ponder how you'd like to combine different yarns for your own unique creations!

REVERSIBLE SLIP STITCH

Stripes and dots are created using slipped stitches and three colors. This pattern is easier to memorize than it looks. Have fun trying different color combinations!

FINISHED MEASUREMENTS
5.5" x 67"/14cm x 170cm

YARN
Berroco Vintage (50% acrylic, 40% wool, 10% nylon; 217 yd/198m per 100g skein) (for substitution purposes, 20 sts = 4"/10cm as per ball band)
- Color A: #5176, Pumpkin; 1 ball
- Color B: #5194, Breezeway; 1 ball
- Color C: #5102, Buttercream; 1 ball

Or approximately 130 yards each of three colors worsted weight yarn.

NEEDLES & NOTIONS
1 US #9/5.5mm circular needle, 20"/50cm or longer
Tapestry needle

GAUGE
21 sts = 4"/10 cm in pattern stitch, after blocking

PATTERN NOTES
The color sequences are listed to help keep track of where you are in the pattern. The "setup" section and first sequence in the beginning get the colors set up so that they will present themselves in the right order for the first, second, and third sequence throughout.

Be sure to carry the yarns up the sides of the scarf by twisting them according to the directions in "Special Terms." Carry the yarns loosely enough to accommodate stretching out during blocking; you don't want them to bind the piece.

To avoid a big tangled mess caused by twisting the yarns together, untwist the balls of yarn frequently.

Pattern stitch is a multiple of 2 sts + 1.

COLOR SEQUENCES
First Sequence:
Rows 1 & 2: Color A
Rows 3 & 4: Color B
Row 5: Color A

Second Sequence:
On row 6, you're starting with the next color that presents itself at the edge of the work you just finished, so Rows 6 & 7: Color C
Rows 8 & 9: Color A
Row 10: Color C

Third Sequence:
Rows 11 & 12: Color B
Rows 13 & 14: Color C
Row 15: Color B

SPECIAL TERMS
Slide: Slide stitches to opposite end of needle and do not turn work.

Twist: Bring old color forward, then upward in front of current yarn. Then move old yarn toward back of work so when you knit with current yarn it is caught.

PATTERN

With Color C and long-tail method, cast on 27 sts.
Setup row: Row 1: Purl. Slide.

Reversible Slip Stitch Pattern:
Row 1: With Color A, knit.
Row 2: With Color A, twist the old and current colors to carry the old up the side. Knit.
Row 3: With Color B, k1, * sl1 wyib, k1; rep from * to end.
Row 4: With Color B, twist. K1, * sl1 wyif, k1; rep from * to end.
Row 5: With Color A, twist. P1, * k1, p1; rep from * to end.
Rows 6-7: With Color C, rep rows 1-2.
Rows 8-9: With Color A, rep rows 3-4.
Row 10: With Color C, rep row 5.
Rows 11-12: With Color B, rep rows 1-2.
Rows 13-14: With Color C, rep rows 3-4.
Row 15: With Color B, rep row 5.
Rep rows 1-15 until scarf measures about 66"/167.5 cm or desired length, ending with row 15.

Ending rows:
Slide sts to other end of needle.
Rows 1-2: With Color C, knit.

Bind off purlwise.

FINISHING

Weave in ends. Block.

RIPPLES

With Ripples I reinterpreted a drop-stitch pattern to make it attractive on both sides. With this versatile pattern, you can play with all kinds of weights and colors. It's beautiful in solids, but also lends itself well to a variegated main color paired with a solid contrast color. See the "Make Your Own" sidebar on the next page for more photos and ideas.

FINISHED MEASUREMENTS

7" x 74"/18cm x 188cm

YARN

Madelinetosh Tosh DK (100% superwash merino wool; 225 yd/206m per 105g skein) (for substitution purposes, 20-22 sts = 4"/10cm as per ball band)
- MC: Warm Maize; 2 skeins
- CC: Saffron; 1 skein

Or approximately 345 yards of MC and 110 yards of CC in DK weight yarn.

NEEDLES & NOTIONS

1 US #5/3.75mm circular needle
Tapestry needle

GAUGE

20 sts/26 rows = 4"/10cm in Ripples Stitch Pattern, after blocking, or
23 sts/30 rows = 4"/10cm in stockinette stitch, after blocking

PATTERN NOTES

Carry the color not being worked neatly up the side of the work by twisting the MC and CC strands around each other at the beginning of rows where both strands are on the same edge of the work.

Pattern stitch is a multiple of 10 sts + 6.

PATTERN

With CC, loosely cast on 36 sts.

Setup rows:
With CC, knit 3 rows.
With MC, knit 1 row. Slide.
With CC, knit 1 row.
With MC, knit 1 row. Slide.
With CC, knit 3 rows.

Ripples Stitch Pattern:
Row 1 (RS): With MC, knit.
Row 2 (WS): With MC, * k1, yo, k1, [yo] twice, k1, [yo] 3 times, k1, [yo] twice, k1, yo, k5; rep from * to last 6 sts, k1, yo, k1, [yo] twice, k1, [yo] 3 times, k1, [yo] twice, k1, yo, k1.
Row 3 (RS): With MC, knit, dropping yo's.
Row 4 (WS): With MC, knit.
Row 5 (RS): With CC, knit. Slide sts to other end of needle, ready to work another RS row.
Row 6 (RS): With MC, knit.
Row 7 (WS): With MC, * k6, yo, k1, [yo] twice, k1, [yo] 3 times, k1, [yo] twice, k1, yo; rep from * to last 6 sts, k6.
Row 8 (RS): With MC, knit, dropping yo's.
Row 9 (WS): With MC, knit. Slide sts to other end of needle, ready to work another WS row.
Row 10 (WS): With CC, knit.
Rep rows 1-10 until piece measures 70"/178cm or desired length (when stretched out as if blocked), ending with row 4.

Ending rows:
With CC, knit 3 rows. Slide.
With MC, purl 1 row.
With CC, knit 1 row. Slide.
With MC, purl 1 row.
With CC, knit 4 rows.

Bind off loosely.

FINISHING

Weave in ends. Wet block, stretching pattern out as for lace to open up the dropped stitches. I like to pin the top and bottom edges to form waves.

MAKE IT YOUR OWN

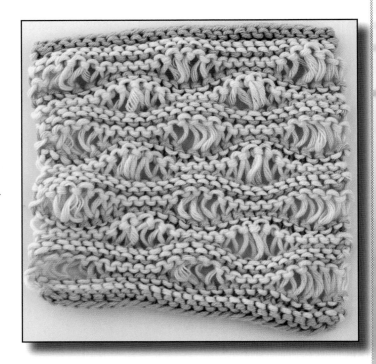

You can easily adapt the Ripples pattern to various yarn weights. If using sock yarn, try casting on 46 or even 56 stitches. For sport, try 36; DK looks good at either 26 or 36, depending on the season you're knitting for. A worsted weight will give you a substantial width perfect for colder weather. Simply stick to a multiple of 10 + 6 stitches.

For an even lacier fabric, try using needles that are two or three sizes larger than what would normally be used for the yarn you've selected. A ribbon, textured, or other novelty yarn paired with a smoother one can create dramatic and fun combinations.

To get just the right look, you can play with the beginning and ending borders – include them, make up your own, or leave them out entirely. Replace some of the MC rows with CC to affect the overall color and impact (just remember to slide the stitches if needed). You'll see by the examples at right that the possibilities are endless!

For a skinny scarf well suited to warmer weather, try casting on 26 stitches using a plant-based fiber such as the unusual 100% corn Kollage Corntastic pictured above right. This will be a fun look, especially if you make it really long.

[Swatch yarns: Kollage Corntastic, Colors #6502, Citrine and #6506, Jade. Photo at top right.]

Ripples also lends itself very well to variegated yarns. Grab that variegated yarn in your stash that's been waiting for the perfect project, pair it with a solid, and you've created a colorful and unexpected accessory. You can play with various solids to see how they affect the other colors. If you have a particularly vibrant variegated yarn, such as the Lorna's Laces Shepherd Worsted pictured here, you can give more prominence to the solid color by substituting some of the CC rows for the MC.

[Swatch yarns: Debbie Bliss Cashmerino Aran, Color #013, Maroon; Lorna's Laces Shepherd Worsted, Color #409, Rockwell. Photo at bottom right.]

STRIPES THREE WAYS

Putting stripes into a project can cause one side to look "wrong." Here are three ways to use stripes that create attractive fabric on both sides. A garter stitch scarf with fringe offers a wonderful framework for mixing yarns in ways that express your unique creativity. This great all-purpose pattern is super easy to knit, but affords you endless possibilities for combining dissimilar yarns together, or holding colors together to produce shading, or using color to create bold stripes. The yarn is cast on lengthwise, and a new length of yarn is started with each row, leaving tails long enough for knotting into fringe at the ends.

A bonus? The long lines created by these patterns look great on most people. (Refer to page 12 in the Techniques chapter for important considerations when casting on lengthwise.) Any of these three techniques – composite, shading, and stripes – can be used horizontally across the width of a scarf, too. In that case, instead of cutting tails each row, the yarn is used as long as it's needed, and the ends woven in.

COMPOSITE STRIPES

Working with several completely different yarns held together makes for a great stash buster. (See main photo at left.) Have fun combining different colors, weights, and textures. Or use one of the novelty yarns called "composites." The manufacturers put several kinds of yarns together into one strand. Or they may put lengths of different strands one after another, knotting them as they change.

Feza Alp Oriental, a composite, uses a riot of yarn types, making it a lot of fun to knit. You'll be working in one set of colors and/or types of yarn, then suddenly it changes to something else entirely. It's like opening up one of those surprise balls that you got as a party favor when you were a kid, and there were little trinkets inside what seemed like miles of crepe paper ribbon – you never knew what you would unravel next.

FINISHED MEASUREMENTS

8" x 64"/20.5cm x 162.5cm, including fringe

YARN

Feza Alp Oriental (30% acrylic, 30% polyamide, 15% mohair, 15% wool, 10% metallic; 165 yd/151m per 325g ball) (for substitution purposes, 9 sts/12 rows = 4"/10cm as per ball band); color: #08, Little Red Riding Hood; 1 ball.

NEEDLES & NOTIONS

1 US #15/10mm circular needle, 47"/120cm or longer
1 US #17/12.75mm circular needle, 47"/120cm or longer
Tapestry needle

GAUGE

8 sts = 4"/10cm in garter stitch

Gauge note: Use your gauge swatch to determine the needle and tension you'll need for casting on and binding off; these are especially important when knitting lengthwise.

PATTERN NOTES

Some novelty yarns, including Alp Oriental, have knots where the different types of yarns are tied together. If you encounter a knot near the beginning of a row, cut it and start the next color or group of fibers that came after the knot. (You will have a small amount of yarn wasted.) If you run across a knot in the middle of the row, cut the knot out, leaving tails on both sides of the knot to weave in later.

To cast on loosely enough, you may want to cast on with larger needles.

PATTERN

Using the larger needles if necessary, and leaving a 6-8"/15-20cm tail to include with fringe, loosely cast on 104 sts. (See "Scarves Worked Lengthwise" section of the Techniques chapter for cast-on suggestions).

At the end of the row, leave a 6-8"/15-20cm tail for fringe, cut yarn.

* Leaving 6-8"/15-20cm of yarn at beginning of the row for fringe, knit to end of row. At the end of the row, leave a 6-8"/15-20cm tail for fringe, cut yarn.

Rep from * until scarf is 7.5"/19cm (it will stretch out for blocking) or desired width.

SHADING
VARIATION

Loosely bind off knitwise, using larger needles if necessary, leaving yarn at each end for fringe.

FINISHING

Separate fringe into groups, taking into consideration the final effect of the different colors and textures. Tie an overhand knot at top of each grouping of fringe, alternating the sides you tie the knots on. Trim fringe evenly to desired length, or unevenly to various different lengths depending on the look you're after. Block.

SHADING

Gradations from dark to light to dark again are created by working with two strands of yarn. Starting off with two strands of the same color, then holding one strand of that color along with a strand of the next lighter or darker color makes the transition from shade to shade. This shaded scarf uses five colors. I like using tweed or heathered yarns to achieve subtle blending.

FINISHED MEASUREMENTS

4" x 76"/10cm x 193cm, including fringe

YARN

Rowan Felted Tweed DK (50% merino wool, 25% alpaca, 25% viscose; 191 yd/175m per 50g ball) (for substitution purposes, 22-24 sts/30-32 rows = 4"/10cm as per ball band); 1 ball each color.
- Color A: #170, Seafarer
- Color B: #178, Seasalter
- Color C: #167, Maritime
- Color D: #165, Scree
- Color E: #177, Clay

NEEDLES & NOTIONS

1 US #10/6mm circular needle, 47"/120cm or longer
Tapestry needle

GAUGE

17sts/30 rows = 4"/10cm in garter stitch with 2 strands held together

Gauge Note: Use your gauge swatch to determine the needle and tension you'll need for casting on and binding off; these are especially important when knitting lengthwise.

PATTERN NOTES

I like to use the cable cast-on technique, followed by a row of knitting through the back loop, to form a uniform edge.

PATTERN

Holding two strands of Color A together, leaving an 8-9"/20-23cm tail to include with fringe, and using the cable-cast on technique, cast on 272 sts. At the end of the row, leave an 8-9"/20-23cm tail for fringe, cut yarn. Slide sts to other end of needle.

Setup row:
Leaving an 8-9"/20-23cm tail at beginning of the row for fringe, ktbl to end of row. At the end of the row, leave an 8-9"/20-23cm tail for fringe, cut yarn. Turn.

Following the stripe sequence below, work each row as follows: Leaving an 8-9"/20-23cm tail at beginning of the row for fringe, knit to end of row. At the end of the row, leave an 8-9"/20-23cm tail for fringe, cut yarn. Turn work and continue as for garter stitch.

Stripe Sequence:
2 rows with 1 strand Color A + 1 strand Color B
2 rows with 2 strands of Color B
2 rows with 1 strand Color B + 1 strand Color C
2 rows with 2 strands of Color C
2 rows with 1 strand Color C + 1 strand Color D
2 rows with 2 strands of Color D
2 rows with 1 strand Color D + 1 strand Color E
2 rows with 2 strands of Color D
2 rows with 1 strand Color D + 1 strand Color C
2 rows with 2 strands of Color C
2 rows with 1 strand Color C + 1 strand Color B
2 rows with 2 strands of Color B
2 rows with 1 strand Color B + 1 strand Color A
1 row with 2 strands of Color A

Using 2 strands of Color A, loosely bind off knitwise, leaving yarn at each end for fringe.

FINISHING

Evenly divide fringe tails into groups. Tie an overhand knot at top of each grouping of fringe, alternating the sides you tie the knots on. Trim fringe to 6"/15cm or desired length. Block.

BOLD STRIPES

In making stripes, when a new color is added, the old color makes little bumps on the purl side. I like using a knit one, purl one technique when changing to a new color, since it looks equally attractive on both sides. For the very narrow stripes, I use a simple slip-stitch technique to weave in an accent color.

While I picked spring colors and a warm-weather cotton for this skinny spring-inspired scarf, you can adapt this pattern for any season, color palette, and type of yarn that you want.

FINISHED MEASUREMENTS
3.5" x 67"/9cm x 170cm

YARN
Tahki Cotton Classic (100% mercerized cotton; 108 yd/100m per 50g skein) (for substitution purposes; 20 sts = 4"/10cm as per ball band); 1 skein each color.
- Color A: #3936, Lavender
- Color B: #3870, Dark Bright Blue
- Color C: #3725, Deep Leaf Green
- Color D: #3534, Pale Yellow
- Color E: #3786, Dark Teal
- Color F: #3928, Light Lavender

NEEDLES & NOTIONS
1 US #5/3.75mm circular needle, 47"/120cm or longer
Tapestry needle

GAUGE
20 sts/28 rows = 4"/10cm in garter stitch

Gauge note: Use your gauge swatch to determine the needle and tension you'll need for casting on and binding off; these are especially important when knitting lengthwise.

PATTERN NOTES
When slipping the stitches for the accent stripes, take care not to pull the yarn too tightly around the stitches. Tension should be adjusted to avoid having the accent stripes pull the fabric in.

To weave in the tails from the slip-stitch accent stripe, use the same idea as the duplicate stitch technique (see Techniques chapter). Using your tapestry needle, weave the tail back over the accent stitches, cutting the end close to the fabric.

PATTERN
With Color A, loosely cast on 360 sts (See "Scarves Worked Lengthwise" section of Techniques chapter for cast-on suggestions).

Row 1: Knit.
Row 2: With Color B, * k1, p1; rep from * to end.
Row 3: Knit.
Row 4: With Color C, * k1, p1; rep from * to end.
Rows 5-7: Knit.
Row 8 (accent stripe): With Color D, * sl1 wyib, sl1 wyif; rep from * to end.
Row 9 (accent stripe): * Sl1 wyif, sl1 wyib; rep from * to end.
Rows 10-12: With Color C, knit.
Row 13: With Color D, * k1, p1; rep from * to end.
Rows 14-16: Knit.
Row 17: With Color E, * k1, p1; rep from * to end.
Rows 18-19: Knit.
Row 20: With Color F, * k1, p1; rep from * to end.
Rows 21-23: Knit.
Row 24 (accent stripe): With Color B, * sl1 wyib, sl1 wyif; rep from * to end.
Row 25 (accent stripe): * Sl1 wyif, sl1 wyib; rep from * to end.
Rows 26-28: With Color F, knit.
Row 29: With Color C, * k1, p1; rep from * to end.
Rows 30-31: Knit.
Row 32 (accent stripe): With Color D, * sl1 wyib, sl1 wyif; rep from * to end.
Row 33 (accent stripe): * Sl1 wyif, sl1 wyib; rep from * to end.
Row 34: With Color C, knit.
Row 35: With Color A, * k1, p1; rep from * to end.
Rows 36-37: Knit.
Bind off loosely knitwise.

FINISHING
Weave in ends. Block.

BOLD
STRIPES
VARIATION

WOVEN DOTS

This scarf works great with either two contrasting solids or a woven variegated on a solid background. I love finding ways to use the luscious variegated yarn in my stash. The dots in this pattern allow for the pretty colors to be shown off, without the pooling that can sometimes be a problem with variegated yarns.

In this pattern the yarn forming the dots is woven back and forth in front of and behind the slipped stitches of the background yarn. The yarn used for the woven rows needs to be thicker than the knitted yarn. So either use a heavier weight – for example, worsted – for the woven yarn with a sport weight for the knitted part, or use the same weight for both the background and the woven element, but double the yarn for the woven part.

FINISHED MEASUREMENTS

7.75" x 70"/19.5cm x 178cm

YARN

Variegated Version:
Color A: Debbie Bliss Baby Cashmerino (55% merino wool, 33% microfiber, 12% cashmere; 137yd/125m per 50g ball) (for substitution purposes, 25 sts/34 rows = 4"/10cm as per ball band); color: #37, Maroon; 5 balls
- Color B: Lorna's Laces Shepherd Worsted (100% superwash wool, 225 yd/206m per 4 oz skein) (for substitution purposes, 18 sts = 4"/10cm as per ball band); color: #105, Glenwood; 1 skein

Solids Version:
- Color A: Debbie Bliss Baby Cashmerino (55% merino wool, 33% microfiber, 12% cashmere; 137yd/125m per 50g ball) (for substitution purposes, 25 sts/34 rows = 4"/10cm as per ball band); color: #300, Black; 5 balls
- Color B: Berroco Vintage (50% acrylic, 50% wool, 217 yd/200m per 3.5 oz/100g skein) (for substitution purposes, 18 sts = 4"/10cm as per ball band); color: #5100, Snow Day; 1 skein

Or for Color A, approximately 685 yards of sport weight yarn; Color B, approximately 230 yards of worsted weight yarn

NEEDLES & NOTIONS

1 US #4/3.5mm circular needle, 16"/40cm or longer
Cable needle
Tapestry needle

GAUGE

24 sts = 4"/10cm in garter stitch with Color A.

Gauge note: Include the I-cord edge to practice getting the tension right, but don't count the I-cord edge sts in your gauge calculations.

PATTERN NOTES

This pattern features I-cord edges. The technique is to knit to the last 4 stitches, leave the yarn in front of your work, then slip the remaining 4 stitches purlwise. When you next knit these stitches from the other side of the work, they will turn away from you and create an I-cord. Be careful not to knit the edge stitches too tightly. You will want to use a tension that allows for tidy I-cord stitches, but at the same time takes into consideration that the edging has to span the woven rows as well. You want the edges of the scarf to be straight, not concave. Including the I-cord edges on your gauge swatch will help you to learn what tension works for you.

Avoid pulling the woven yarn too tightly or the "dots" will be too small.

Color A: The background knitted yarn. Color B: The woven yarn.

Pattern stitch is a multiple of 2 sts, plus 8 edge sts (4 each side).

PATTERN

With Color A, cast on 50 sts (this includes the I-cord edge sts).

Setup rows:
Rows 1-3: With Color A, knit to last 4 sts, sl4 wyif. Turn.
Row 4: With Color A, knit to last 4 sts, sl4 wyif. Slide.
Row 5: With Color B, sl4, * sl1 wyib, sl1 wyif; rep from * to last 4 sts, sl4 wyib. Turn.
Row 6: With Color A, knit to last 4 sts, sl4 wyif. Turn.
Row 7: With Color A, knit to last 4 sts; bring Color B to front; bring Color A to front, laying it over Color B. (This anchors Color B under Color A to set up for the following row.) Without working last 4 sts, turn.
Row 8: Bring Color B from back to front; with Color B, * sl1 wyif, sl1 wyib; rep from * to last 4 sts, sl4 wyif. Slide.

Woven Dots Pattern:
Row 1: With Color A, knit to last 4 sts, sl4 wyif. Turn.
Row 2: With Color A, k4, bring Color B to front; with Color A, knit to last 4 sts, sl4 wyif. Slide.
Row 3: Sl4, bring Color B to the back; with Color B, * sl1 wyib, sl1 wyif; rep from * to last 4 sts, sl4 wyib. Turn.
Row 4: With Color A, knit to last 4 sts, sl4 wyif. Turn.
Row 5: With Color A, knit to last 4 sts; bring Color B to front; bring Color A to front, laying it over Color B (this anchors Color B under Color A to set up for the following row). Without working last 4 sts, turn.
Row 6: Bring Color B from back to front; with Color B, * sl1 wyif, sl1 wyib; rep from * to last 4 sts, ending yf, sl4. Slide.
Rep rows 1-6 until piece measures 69.5"/176.5cm or desired length, ending with row 6.

Ending rows:
Rows 1-4: With Color A, knit to last 4 sts, sl4 wyif. Turn.

Binding off:
Bind off to last 4 sts (you will have 1 st on right-hand needle, 4 on left-hand needle). Keep yarn in back of work and sl4 left-hand needle sts onto cable needle. Twist the cable needle toward you to mimic the twist of the I-cord. Bind off remaining sts from cable needle.

FINISHING
Weaving in ends: At the top and bottom edges, you'll have ends from the cast-on and bind-off. Weave them in along top/bottom edge, using them to secure I-cord in place.

Weave in all other ends. Block.

CHAPTER 4: CABLES AND RIBS IN REVERSE

Using cables and ribs, either on their own or in combination, creates designs with wide appeal. This chapter offers up several ways to make reversible patterns incorporating cables and ribs.

If you're planning on making a scarf for a man, the Braided Cables pattern offers substantial but different cables on each side. Or maybe you'd like the scarf to be the same on each side? The Aran pattern uses ribbing to form the same cable on both sides. It's a wonderful technique to have in your repertoire, and you can easily use it to create your own designs.

Finally, we have one of my favorite styles – using cables on one side of the scarf, and lacey ribs on the other. Each side is stunning but different.

ARAN

This pattern looks complex, but in reality is very easy. With only two rows of instructions making up the six-row pattern repeat, it's simple to memorize and fun to work. Using a ribbed reverse cable technique made popular by Lily Chin and others, ribs are formed on both sides of the scarf simultaneously as you go along. Rowan's Cashsoft 4 Ply has just the right combination of softness, loft, drape, and stitch definition to make this scarf both eye-catching and flexible, despite the ribs' thickness.

FINISHED MEASUREMENTS
7.25" x 68"/18.5cm x 172.5cm

YARN
Rowan Cashsoft 4 Ply (57% extrafine merino wool, 33% acrylic microfiber, 10% cashmere; 197 yd/180m per 50g ball) (for substitution purposes, 28 sts/36 rows = 4"/10cm as per ball band); color: #453, Cherish; 6 balls.

Or approximately 890 yards of fingering weight yarn

NEEDLES & NOTIONS
1 pair US #6/4mm straight needles
Cable needle
Tapestry needle
Removable stitch marker (optional)

GAUGE
24 sts/30 rows = 4"/10cm in stockinette stitch

PATTERN NOTES
Increases and decreases are used at the top and bottom of the work to minimize the flaring that can occur at the beginning and end of cables.

It's easy to get confused about which side of the scarf you're working. Keep track of which side you're on by placing a removable stitch marker on the side of your work with the odd-numbered rows. Or jot down which side of your needle the tail from your cast-on is on when you start an odd-numbered row.

SPECIAL ABBREVIATIONS
M1 (knitwise, on side 2): In bar between stitches, insert left needle from front to back; knit this loop through the back

C8B (Cable 8 Back): Slip next 4 sts onto cable needle and hold to back of work; [k1, p1] twice from left-hand needle, [k1, p1] twice from cable needle.

C8F (Cable 8 Front): Slip next 4 sts onto cable needle and hold to front of work; [k1, p1] twice from left-hand needle, [k1, p1] twice from cable needle.

C12B (Cable 12 Back): Slip next 6 sts onto cable needle and hold to back of work; [k1, p1] 3 times from left-hand needle, [k1, p1] 3 times from cable needle.

C12F (Cable 12 Front): Slip next 6 sts onto cable needle and hold to front of work; [k1, p1] 3 times from left-hand needle, [k1, p1] 3 times from cable needle.

PATTERN

Cast on 50 sts.
Setup row: K1, p1, k6, p1, k1, [k1, p1] twice, k23, [p1, k1] 3 times, k5, p1, k1.

Increase row: K1, p1, k1, [m1, p1] 4 times, k1, p1, k1, [k1, p1] twice, k5, [m1, p1] 12 times, k6, [p1, k1] 3 times, [m1, p1] 4 times, k1, p1, k1. [70 sts]

Reversible Aran Stitch Pattern:
Row 1: K1, p1, k1, [k1, p1] 4 times, k1, p1, k1, [k1, p1] twice, k5, [k1, p1] 12 times, k5, [k1, p1] 3 times, k1, [k1, p1] 4 times, k1, p1, k1.
Row 2: Rep row 1.
Row 3: K1, p1, k1, C8F, k1, p1, k1, [k1, p1] twice, k5, C12B, C12F, k5, [k1, p1] 3 times, k1, C8B, k1, p1, k1.
Rows 4-6: Rep row 1.

Rep rows 1-6, ending with row 6, until scarf measures 68"/172.5cm or desired length.

Bind off with decreases as follows: Bind off 4 sts, [k2tog, pass 1 st over] 3 times, bind off 5 sts, k2tog, pass 1 st over, bind off 7 sts, [k2tog, pass 1 st over] 11 times, bind off 7 sts, k2tog, pass 1 st over, bind off 5 sts, [k2tog, pass 1 st over] 3 times, bind off to end.

FINISHING

Weave in ends. You may find you don't need to block this scarf at all. But if you do, block without stretching it.

REVERSIBLE ARAN STITCH PATTERN CHART
As seen from side 1

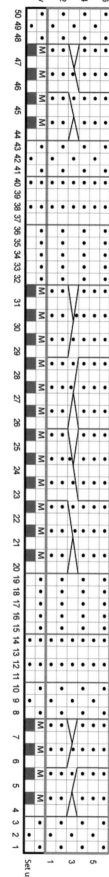

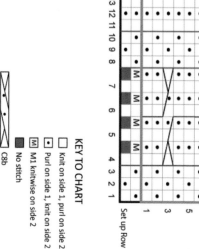

C12f
C12b
C8f
C8b

KEY TO CHART

☐	Knit on side 1, purl on side 2
•	Purl on side 1, knit on side 2
Ⓜ	M1 knitwise on side 2
■	No stitch

MAKE IT YOUR OWN

Reversible rib-and-cable patterns are among my favorites. Their variety of stitches keeps me entertained, yet at the same time they can be easy to memorize.

To create your own patterns, start by browsing stitch dictionaries to find cables, ribs, and lacy ribs that appeal to you. Because you will see the back side of each rib or cable, take each one's width into consideration. I prefer rib patterns that have only a few stitches across, as I like the way they look better from the opposite side.

When you find stitch patterns you like, play with combinations of appealing repeats until you achieve the look you want.

If your design includes a cable or rib at the edge of your scarf, keep in mind that it may have a tendency to fold over along its knit side. You can cure this problem by including a reverse stockinette (i.e., purl) stitch next to it. (You can see how it's used in my Double Eyelet and Cables design, page 91, which uses this method to make the scarf lie flat.)

Your creation will be affected by the yarn you choose. A worsted weight makes a great scarf to dress down with jeans in cooler weather. A thinner yarn can create a dressier mood, or provide an accent in warm weather.

BRAIDED CABLE SCARF

Using bulky yarn, this project is quick to knit. Attractive on both sides, a subtle but fun feature is that the cables aim in one direction on one side of the scarf, and the other direction on the other side. With only four rows in the cable repeat, it's easy to memorize the pattern.

FINISHED MEASUREMENTS

6" x 66"/15cm x 167.5cm

YARN

Lorna's Laces Shepherd Bulky (100% superwash wool; 140 yd/128m per 113g skein) (for substitution purposes, 14 sts = 4"/10cm as per ball band); color: #9ns, Pewter; 3 skeins

Or approximately 320 yards of bulky weight yarn

NEEDLES & NOTIONS

1 pair US #10.5/6.5mm straight needles
Cable needle
Tapestry needle

GAUGE

19 sts = 4"/10cm in pattern stitch, after blocking without flattening the cables

PATTERN NOTE

Cable charts (see next page) are provided for visual reference. Chart A represents the cables on Side 1 of the scarf; Chart B represents the cable on Side 2.

SPECIAL ABBREVIATIONS

C4F (Cable 4 Front): Slip next 2 sts onto cable needle and hold to front of work; k2 from left-hand needle, then k2 from cable needle.

C4B (Cable 4 Back): Slip next 2 sts onto cable needle and hold at back of work; k2 from left-hand needle, then k2 from cable needle.

PATTERN

Using a long-tail knit/purl cast-on (see the Techniques chapter for instructions), cast on 28 sts as follows: P3, k2, p6, k6, p6, k2, p3.

Setup rows:
Row 1: K1, p1, k1, p2, k6, p6, k6, p2, k1, p1, k1.
Row 2: K1, p1, k3, p6, k6, p6, k3, p1, k1.

Braided Cable Pattern:
Row 1 (side 1): K1, p1, k1, p2, k2, C4F, p6, k2, C4F, p2, k1, p1, k1.
Row 2 (side 2): K1, p1, k3, p6, k2, C4B, p6, k3, p1, k1.
Row 3: K1, p1, k1, p2, C4B, k2, p6, C4B, k2, p2, k1, p1, k1.
Row 4: K1, p1, k3, p6, C4F, k2, p6, k3, p1, k1.
Rep rows 1-4 until scarf measures 66"/167.5cm or desired length, ending with row 4.

Ending row (side 1): K1, p1, k1, p2, k6, p6, k6, p2, k1, p1, k1.

Bind off in pattern.

FINISHING

Weave in ends. Block without stretching.

CABLE CHART A
Panel of 6 sts, as seen from side 1.

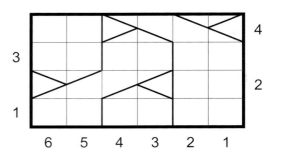

CABLE CHART B
Panel of 6 sts, as seen from side 2.

KEY TO CHARTS

Knit on side 1, purl on side 2

C4F = cable 4 front

C4B = cable 4 back

SIDE 1   SIDE 2

CABLES AND KNOTS

Jaunty cables form a scalloped edge on this scarf. Cables on both sides make it reversible. This scarf is as cheery to knit as it is to wear.

FINISHED MEASUREMENTS
4.25" x 70"/11cm x 178cm

YARN
Debbie Bliss Cashmerino Aran (55% merino wool, 33% microfibre, 12% cashmere; 99 yd/90m per 50g ball) (for substitution purposes, 18 sts = 4"/10cm as per ball band); color: #502, Pea Green; 5 balls.

Or approximately 410 yards of worsted weight yarn

NEEDLES & NOTIONS
1 pair US #6/4mm straight needles
Cable needle
Tapestry needle

GAUGE
33 sts = 4"/10cm in pattern stitch, after blocking, or
20 sts = 4"/10cm stockinette stitch, after blocking

PATTERN NOTE
Pattern stitch is a multiple of 10 sts + 5.

SPECIAL ABBREVIATIONS
C5 (Cable 5): Slip next 3 sts onto cable needle and hold at back of work; k2 from left-hand needle, then k3 from cable needle.

MK (Make Knot): (K1, p1, k1, p1, k1) into next st. Counting from the tip of your right-hand needle, you'll have the working (first) st, then the 2nd, 3rd, 4th and 5th sts that will form your knot. With your left-hand needle, skip the first st, and one at a time pass the 2nd, then 3rd, 4th, and 5th sts over the first st. Voila! Your knot is complete.

PATTERN
Using a long-tail knit/purl cast-on (see the Techniques chapter for instructions), cast on 35 sts as follows: [P5, k5] 3 times, p5.

Setup rows:
Row 1: * K5, p5; rep from * to last 5 sts, k5.
Row 2: * P5, k5; rep from * to last 5 sts, p5.
Rows 3, 5 & 7: Rep row 1.
Rows 4 & 6: Rep row 2.
Row 8: * P5, C5; rep from * to last 5 sts, p5.
Row 9: * K5, p5; rep from * to last 5 sts, k5.
Row 10: * P5, k5; rep from * to last 5 sts, p5.

Cables and Knots Pattern:
Row 1: * C5, p5; rep from * to last 5 sts, C5.
Row 2: * P5, k2, MK, k2; rep from * to last 5 sts, p5.
Row 3: * K5, p5; rep from * to last 5 sts, k5.
Row 4: * P5, k5; rep from * to last 5 sts, p5.
Row 5: * K2, MK, k2, p5; rep from * to last 5 sts, k2, MK, k2.
Row 6: * P5, C5; rep from * to last 5 sts, p5.
Row 7: * K5, p5; rep from * to last 5 sts, k5.
Row 8: * P5, k5; rep from * to last 5 sts, p5.
Rep rows 1-8 until scarf measures 69"/175.5cm, or 1"/2.5 cm less than desired length, ending with row 8.

Ending rows:
Row 1: * C5, p5; rep from * to last 5 sts, C5.
Row 2: * P5, k5; rep from * to last 5 sts, p5.
Row 3: * K5, p5; rep from * to last 5 sts, k5.
Rep rows 2 and 3 two more times.

Bind off in pattern.

FINISHING
Weave in ends. Block without stretching.

DIAGONAL RIBS AND LITTLE FOUNTAINS LACE

The lace in this scarf, truly reminiscent of the little fountains it is named for, is easy to knit but with elegant results. The diagonal ribs are a lovely replacement for cables, and are made without the need for a cable needle. This is a great pattern for beginning knitters who would like to master some intermediate techniques.

FINISHED MEASUREMENTS
6" x 70"/15cm x 178cm

YARN
Lorna's Laces Shepherd Sport (100% superwash wool; 200 yd/183m per 70g skein) (for substitution purposes, 24 sts = 4"/10cm as per ball band); color: #51ns, Island Blue; 2 skeins.

Or approximately 360 yards of sport weight yarn

NEEDLES & NOTIONS
1 pair US 4/3.5mm straight needles
Tapestry needle

GAUGE
26 sts/32 rows = 4"/10cm in pattern stitch, after blocking

PATTERN NOTES
Keep first and last 2 sts of each row in garter stitch throughout pattern for edging.

Pattern stitch is a multiple of 10 sts + 5, plus 4 edge sts (2 each side).

SPECIAL ABBREVIATION
LT (Left Twist): Skip the first st on the left-hand needle. With the right-hand needle behind the left one, knit the second st on the left-hand needle through the back loop. The newly knitted st will be on your right-hand needle. Slip the skipped st purlwise onto right-hand needle, dropping the newly knitted st off the left-hand needle as usual.

PATTERN
Cast on 39 sts.

Setup rows:
Rows 1-3: Knit.
Row 4: K2, p5, * k5, p5; rep from * to last 2 sts, k2.

Little Fountains Lace Pattern:
Row 1: K3, yo, k3, yo, k1, * p5, k1, yo, k3, yo, k1; rep from * to last 2 sts, k2.
Row 2: K2, p7, * LT, k3, p7; rep from * to last 2 sts, k2.
Row 3: K4, SK2P, k2,* p5, K2, SK2P, k2; rep from * to last 2 sts, k2.
Row 4: K2, p5, * k1, LT, k2, p5; rep from * to last 2 sts, k2.
Row 5: K3, yo, k3, yo, k1; * p5, k1, yo, k3, yo, k1; rep from * to last 2 sts, k2.
Row 6: K2, p7, * k2, LT, k1, p7; rep from * to last 2 sts, k2.
Row 7: K4, SK2P, k2, * p5, k2, SK2P, k2; rep from * to last 2 sts, k2.
Row 8: K2, p5, * k3, LT, p5; rep from * to last 2 sts, k2.
Rep rows 1-8 until piece measures nearly 70"/178cm or desired length, ending with row 8.

Ending rows:
Row 1: K7, * p5, k5; rep from * to last 2 sts, k2.
Rows 2 & 3: Knit.

Bind off knit-wise.

FINISHING
Weave in ends. Block with lace side down to preserve the texture of the ribs.

DOUBLE EYELET AND CABLES SCARF

Graceful double eyelet lace on one side and ribs on the other make this scarf reversible. The ruffle lends a fun, feminine touch.

FINISHED MEASUREMENTS
6" x 74"/15cm x 188cm

YARN
Karabella Aurora 8 (100% extrafine merino wool; 98 yd/90m per 50g ball) (for substitution purposes, 18 sts = 4"/10cm as per ball band); color: #262, Cantaloupe; 6 skeins.

Or approximately 430 yards of worsted weight yarn

NEEDLES & NOTIONS
1 pair US #8/5mm straight needles
Cable needle
Removable stitch marker
Tapestry needle

GAUGE
24.5 sts/28 rows = 4"/10cm in Double Eyelet and Cables Pattern, after wet blocking without flattening cables

PATTERN NOTES
Ruffle is a multiple of 17 sts + 8, plus 6 edge sts (3 each side).

Double Eyelet & Cables Pattern is a multiple of 9 sts + 4, plus 6 edge sts (3 each side).

SPECIAL ABBREVIATIONS
C4F (Cable 4 Front): Slip next 2 sts onto cable needle and hold at front of work; k2 from left-hand needle, then k2 from cable needle.

M1R (Make 1 Right): At the point where you want to make the increase, lift the running strand of yarn between the two sts with the left-hand needle, inserting needle from back to front. Knit the lifted yarn as if it were a st.

M1L (Make 1 Left): At the point where you want to make the increase, lift the running strand of yarn between the two sts with the left-hand needle, inserting needle from front to back. Knit the lifted yarn through the back loop.

PATTERN
Using a long-tail knit/purl cast-on (see the Techniques chapter for instructions), loosely cast on 65 sts as follows: K3, p8, [k9, p8] 3 times, k3.

Beginning Ruffle:
Row 1 (side 1): K1, p2, k8, * p9, k8; rep from * to last 3 sts, p2, k1.
Row 2 (side 2): K1, p1, k1, p8, * k9, p8; rep from * to last 3 sts, k1, p1, k1.
Rep these 2 rows until ruffle measures 1.5"/4cm (approx 5 repeats) or desired length from cast-on edge, ending with row 2.

Ruffle Decrease:
Row 1 (side 1): K1, p2, ssk, k4, k2tog, * p9, ssk, k4, k2tog; rep from * to last 3 sts, p2, k1. [57 sts.]
Row 2 (side 2): K1, p1, k1, p6, * [ssk] twice, k1, [k2tog] twice, p6; rep from * to last 3 sts, k1, p1, k1. [45 sts.]
Row 3 (side 1): K1, p2, ssk, k2, k2tog, * p5, ssk, k2, k2tog; rep from * to last 3 sts, p2, k1. [37 sts.]
Row 4: K1, p1, k1, p4, * k5, p4; rep from * to last 3 sts, k1, p1, k1.

Double Eyelet and Cables Pattern:
Row 1 (side 1): K1, p2, k4, * p5, k4; rep from * to last 3 sts, p2, k1.
Row 2 (side 2): K1, p1, k1, p4, * k2tog, yo, k1, yo, ssk, p4; rep from * to last 3 sts, k1, p1, k1.
Row 3: K1, p2, k4, * p5, k4; rep from * to last 3 sts, p2, k1.
Row 4: K1, p1, k1, p4, * k5, p4; rep from * to last 3 sts, k1, p1, k1.
Row 5: K1, p2, C4F, * p5, C4F; rep from * to last 3 sts, p2, k1.
Row 6: K1, p1, k1, p4, * k2tog, yo, k1, yo, ssk, p4; rep from * to last 3 sts, k1, p1, k1.
Row 7: K1, p2, k4, * p5, k4; rep from * to last 3 sts, p2, k1.
Row 8: K1, p1, k1, p4, * k5, p4; rep from * to last 3 sts, k1, p1, k1.
Rep rows 1-8 until piece measures 72"/183cm from cast-on edge, or 2"/5cm less than desired length, ending with row 8.

Ruffle Increase:
Row 1 (side 1): K1, p2, k1, m1R, k2, m1L, k1, * p5, k1, m1R, k2, m1L, k1; rep from * to last 3 sts, p2, k1. [45 sts.]
Row 2 (side 2): K1, p1, k1, p6, * [k1, m1R] twice, k1, [k1, m1L] twice, k1, p6; rep from * to last 3 sts, k1, p1, k1. [57 sts.]
Row 3: K1, p2, k1, m1R, k4, m1L, k1, * p9, k1, m1R, k4, m1L, k1; rep from * to last 3 sts, p2, k1. [65 sts.]
Row 4: K1, p1, k1, p8, * k9, p8; rep from * to last 3 sts, k1, p1, k1.
Mark row with marker for purposes of measuring length of ruffle later.

Ending Ruffle:
Row 1 (side 1): K1, p2, k8, * p9, k8; rep from * to last 3 sts, p2, k1.
Row 2 (side 2): K1, p1, k1, p8, * k9, p8; rep from * to last 3 sts, k1, p1, k1.
Rep these 2 rows until ruffle measures 1.5"/4cm (approx. 5 repeats) or desired length from row marker, ending with row 2.

Bind off in pattern.

FINISHING
Weave in ends. Block with lace side down to preserve the texture of the ribs.

WAVY RIBS

The traditional version of the Wavy Ribs stitch pattern looks good on only one side. Here's a perfect example of how a stitch pattern can be modified to look great on both sides. I love its jaunty look!

FINISHED MEASUREMENTS
5.5" x 68"/14cm x 172.5cm

YARN
Debbie Bliss Cashmerino Aran (55% merino wool, 33% acrylic microfibre, 12% cashmere; 99 yd/90m per 50g ball) (for substitution purposes, 18 sts = 4"/10cm as per ball band); color: #37, Raspberry; 5 balls.

Or approximately 380 yards of worsted weight yarn

NEEDLES & NOTIONS
1 pair US #7/4.5mm straight needles
1 pair US #8/5mm straight needles
Tapestry needle

GAUGE
28 sts = 4"/10cm in Wavy Ribs Pattern on larger needles, after blocking

PATTERN NOTES
Wavy Ribs Pattern is a multiple of 4 sts + 2.

SPECIAL ABBREVIATIONS
Note: even some experienced knitters find these cross stitches confusing. For more details, including a link to a YouTube demonstration, see the Techniques Chapter.

C2F (Cross 2 Front): This will cause the next stitch to cross to the front of the following stitch. Skip the first st on the left-hand needle and knit the second st though the back loop and leave it on the needle. Twist the right-hand needle to the front of the work and knit the skipped st through the front loop. Slip both sts off the needle.

C2B (Cross 2 Back): This will cause the next stitch to cross behind the following stitch. Skip the first st on the left-hand needle and knit the second st through the front loop and leave it on the needle. Knit the skipped st through the front loop, then slip both sts off the needle together.

PATTERN
Using smaller needles and a long-tail knit/purl cast-on (see the Techniques chapter for instructions), cast on 38 sts as follows: K1, [k2, p2] 9 times, k1.

Beginning Ribbing:
Row 1 (RS): P1tbl, * k2, p2; rep from * to last st, p1tbl.
Row 2 (WS): K1tbl, * k2, p2; rep from * to last st, k1tbl.
Rep these 2 rows 5 times more for a total of 12 rows. Rep row 1 once more.

Wavy Ribs Pattern:
Switch to larger needles.
Row 1 (WS): K1tbl, * C2F, p2; rep from * to last st, k1tbl.
Row 2: P1tbl, * C2F, p2; rep from * to last st, p1tbl.
Row 3: K1tbl, * C2B, p2; rep from * to last st, k1tbl.
Row 4: P1tbl, * C2B, p2; rep from * to last st, p1tbl.
Rep rows 1-4 until scarf measures 66"/167.5cm or 2"/5cm less than desired length, ending with row 4.

Ending Ribbing:
Switch to smaller needles.
Row 1 (WS): K1tbl, * k2, p2; rep from * to last st, k1tbl.
Row 2 (RS): P1tbl, * k2, p2; rep from * to last st, p1tbl.
Rep these 2 rows 5 times more for a total of 12 rows.
Bind off in pattern.

FINISHING
Weave in ends. Block, being careful to preserve the texture of the ribs.

CHAPTER 5: TWICE THE FUN WITH DOUBLE-KNITTING

Double-knitting creates two pieces of connected, back-to-back fabric at the same time, making it ideal for reversible scarves. Some of the scarves presented here, such as Checkerboard, have patterns that are the same on both sides but with opposite colors. The Surprise Stripes scarf, on the other hand, has stripes running horizontally on one side and vertically on the other. Quite the surprise, indeed!

Two common techniques for working double-knitting are the slip-stitch method and the two-stranded method. The slip-stitch method is well within the skill set of most knitters. The two-stranded method, on the other hand, requires knitting with two strands at once, whether both in one hand or one color in each hand. So that you don't have to learn a new technique, I've written the double-knitting patterns using the slip-stitch method on a circular needle. You work each row twice, once for each color. With each row worked, you'll be forming knit stitches on the front of your work and purl stitches that create the pattern on the "back" of your work. If this sounds complicated, you might want to start with the simplest pattern, Duplicity. It forms two pieces of knitting, joined only at the edges.

A good tool for keeping your place (and your sanity) is a sticky note or magnetic strip placed underneath the written directions. Or if you're following a chart, position the place marker above the row you're working on so you can visually compare your work to the chart. You'll soon get the hang of double-knitting.

To weave in ends, use the duplicate stitch method shown in the Techniques section, then hide the end between layers of your double-knitting.

CHECKERBOARD

This pattern's simple repeats make it an ideal one to start with if you haven't tried double-knitting before.

FINISHED MEASUREMENTS
6" x 65"/15cm x 165cm

YARN
RYC Cashsoft DK (57% extrafine merino wool, 33% acrylic microfibre, 10% cashmere; 142 yd/130m per 50g ball) (for substitution purposes, 22 sts/30 rows = 4"/10cm as per ball band)

- Color A: #519 Black; 5 balls
- Color B: #517 Donkey; 3 balls
- Color C: #507 Savannah; 3 balls

Or approximately 700 yards Color A, 400 yards Color B, and 400 yards of Color C in dk weight yarn

NEEDLES & NOTIONS
1 US #3/3.25mm circular needle or 1 pair US #3/3.25mm straight needles
1 US #5/3.75mm circular needle
Tapestry needle

GAUGE
36 sts/28 rows = 4"/10cm in pattern stitch on larger needles, after blocking

Gauge notes: Remember that with double-knitting, you only see half the total number of stitches as you look at one side of the double fabric. So to get 36 sts per 4"/10cm, you will see 18 sts on one side (the other 18 sts are on the other side).

Use your gauge swatch to work out what size needle will work for you for the cast-on and bind-off. The end of your swatch (and eventually your scarf) should be straight – neither flared nor pulled in.

PATTERN NOTES

The instructions include a slipped selvedge stitch on each side. In order to maintain the slipped-stitch selvedge in Color A, be careful not to wrap Color B or Color C around the end of the row. Always keep them to the inside of the slipped-stitch selvedge. The open ends formed by the edging will be less noticeable once the scarf is blocked.

Pattern stitch is a multiple of 12 sts + 6, plus 2 edge sts (1 each side).

PATTERN

Using smaller needles, Color A, and a long-tail knit/purl cast-on (see the Techniques chapter for instructions), cast on 56 sts as follows: K1, * p1, k1; rep from * to last st, k1.

Change to larger needles and work the pattern as follows:
Row 1: With Color A, sl1 wyif, * [k1, sl1 wyif] 3 times, [sl1 wyib, p1] 3 times; rep from * to last 7 sts, [k1, sl1 wyif] 3 times, k1. Turn.
Row 2: With Color B, sl1 wyif, * [k1, sl1 wyif] 3 times, [sl1 wyib, p1] 3 times; rep from * to last 7 sts, [k1, sl1 wyif] 3 times, sl1 wyib. Slide.
Row 3: With Color A, sl1 wyif, * [sl1 wyib, p1] 3 times, [k1, sl1 wyif] 3 times; rep from * to last 7 sts, [sl1 wyib, p1] 3 times, k1. Turn.
Row 4: With Color B, sl1 wyif, * [sl1 wyib, p1] 3 times, [k1, sl1 wyif] 3 times; rep from * to last 7 sts, [sl1 wyib, p1] 3 times, sl1 wyib. Slide.
Rows 5-8: Rep rows 1-4.

Note: Starting with the next row, the box colors will change.

Row 9: With Color A, sl1 wyif, * [sl1 wyib, p1] 3 times, [k1, sl1 wyif] 3 times; rep from * to last 7 sts, [sl1 wyib, p1] 3 times, k1. Turn.
Row 10: With Color B, sl1 wyif, * [sl1 wyib, p1] 3 times, [k1, sl1 wyif] 3 times; rep from * to last 7 sts, [sl1 wyib, p1] 3 times, sl1 wyib. Slide.
Row 11: With Color A, sl1 wyif, * [k1, sl1 wyif] 3 times, [sl1 wyib, p1] 3 times; rep from * to last 7 sts, [k1, sl1 wyif] 3 times, k1. Turn.
Row 12: With Color B, sl1 wyif, * [k1, sl1 wyif] 3 times, [sl1 wyib, p1] 3 times; rep from * to last 7 sts, [k1, sl1 wyif] 3 times, sl1 wyib. Slide.
Rows 13-16: Rep rows 9-12.
Rep rows 1-16 another 3 times.

Using Color C in place of Color B, work rows 1-16 four times.

Continue as above, alternating Colors B and C, until piece measures 64"/162.5cm or desired length, ending with row 16.

Ending row: With Color A, k1, * k1, p1; rep from * to last st, k1.

Change to smaller needles and bind off as follows: K2, p1, pass first st over next 2 sts, k1, pass first st over next 2 sts, p1, pass first st over next 2 sts, and continue in pattern until there are 2 sts left. Pass the first st over the last st and pull the yarn tail through the last st.

FINISHING

Weave in ends. Block scarf without stretching.

DUPLICITY

This scarf features a printed sock yarn (sometimes called "jacquard") on one side and a solid color on the other. It's the perfect pattern for beginning double-knitters, as it's simple stockinette on each side.

FINISHED MEASUREMENTS
6" x 74"/15cm x 188cm

YARN

- MC: Knit Picks Stroll (75% superwash merino wool, 25% nylon; 231 yd/211m per 50g ball) (for substitution purposes, 28-32 sts = 4"/10cm as per ball band); color: #25025, Aurora Heather; 2 balls.
- CC: Berroco Comfort Sock (50% superfine nylon, 50% superfine acrylic; 447 yd/412m per 100g ball) (for substitution purposes, 30 sts = 4"/10cm as per ball band); color: #1815, Fruit Cocktail; 1 ball.

Or approximately 465 yards of solid-colored sock yarn for MC and approximately 455 yards of printed (jacquard) sock yarn for CC. You may need one extra skein to achieve the full 78" depending on your knitting tension; purchase extra if your LYS allows returns and exchanges, just in case!

NEEDLES & NOTIONS
1 US #1/2.25mm circular needle or 1 pair US #1/2.25mm straight needles
1 US #2/2.75mm circular needle
Tapestry needle

GAUGE
48 sts = 4"/10cm in pattern stitch on larger needles, after blocking

Gauge notes: Remember that with double-knitting, you only see half the number of stitches as you look at one side of the double fabric. So to get 48 sts per 4"/10cm, you will see 24 sts on one side (the other 24 sts are on the other side).

Use your gauge swatch to work out what size needle will work for you for the cast-on and bind-off. The end of your swatch (and eventually your scarf) should be straight – neither flared nor pulled in.

PATTERN NOTES
There are 3 edge stitches on each side, 2 garter stitches and 1 slipped stitch. To form the slipped stitch edge, slip the first stitch purlwise with yarn in front, then bring yarn to back. Keep the slipped edge stitch somewhat loose so edge doesn't pull inward.

Pattern stitch is a multiple of 2 sts, plus 6 edge sts (3 each side).

PATTERN
With smaller needles and MC, cast on 68 sts; cast on first 3 and last 3 edge sts loosely.

Setup rows: Row 1: With larger needles and MC, k3, * k1, p1; rep from * to last 3 sts, k3. Row 2: Sl1, k2, * k1, p1; rep from * to last 3 sts, k3.

Pattern rows:
Row 1: Sl3 edge sts, then with CC, * k1, sl1 wyif; rep from * to last 3 sts, wyib sl3 edge sts. Slide.
Row 2: With MC, sl1, k2, * sl1 wyib, p1; rep from * to last 3 sts, k3. Turn.
Row 3: Sl3 edge sts, then with CC, * sl1 wyib, p1; rep from * to last 3 sts, wyif sl3 edge sts. Slide.
Row 4: With MC, sl1, k2, * k1, sl1 wyif; rep from * to last 3 sts, k3. Turn.
Rep rows 1-4 until scarf measures approx 74"/188cm or desired length, ending with row 4.

Ending rows:
Note: On the next row you will knit the CC knit sts and slip the MC purl sts.
Row 1: With MC, sl1, k2, * k1, sl1 wyif; rep from * to last 3 sts, k3. Turn.
Rep this row 2 more times.

Special bind-off:
Note: This recommended bind-off is a good one for double-knitting. Adjust your tension in order to work the edge stitches very loosely so they don't pull inward as compared to the double-knitted stitches. Unlike a typical bind-off, you will pass the stitch over 2 sts, rather than the usual 1 st.

With MC, k3 loosely, pass first st over next 2 sts to bind off, then resuming normal tension, * k1, bind off first st over next 2 sts, p1, bind off 1 st over 2 sts; rep from * to last 3 sts, knit and bind off these 3 sts in pattern.

When 2 sts remain, cut yarn and draw the tail through both sts to finish.

FINISHING

Weave in ends. Block carefully, avoiding wrinkles.

MAKE IT YOUR OWN

At its most basic, double-knitting forms two pieces of stockinette, joined only by the stitches at the edges if edge stitches are included (otherwise, the sides are open). You can use Duplicity as a jumping off point for creating your own look. Maybe you'd like to use a different solid on each side of your scarf. Or use several colors to make horizontal stripes. Or try a variegated.

For all-over stitch patterns, look online or in books for stitch combinations you'd like to apply to your own scarf design. These instructions are often written out line by line.

You might want to create your own design using a chart. Motifs can be symmetrical, in which case their shape will be the same on both sides of the scarf. The same chart could be used for both sides. If a motif is not symmetrical, the opposite side is a mirror image and you'll need to flip the chart horizontally for the opposite side. The charts are flipped vertically for the end of the scarf. You can get an idea about how to do this by studying the Sprouts design (page 105).

When charting, I like to use proportional squares. The stitches are usually wider than they are tall, so I use a charting software, grid printing software, or even spreadsheet software to make graphs that represent the final design. I also find it helpful to put heavier lines every five squares or so. It makes keeping track of my place in the chart much easier! (See the Resources section for proportional software and proportional grid paper).

Because the fabric created by double-knitting is thicker than usual, I like to use yarn that has good drape. I tend to stick with DK or lighter weight yarn for the same reason. To show off your pattern, use colors with a lot of contrast.

Double-knitting tends to be loose if you use the yarn manufacturer's suggested needle size; you may end up seeing too much of the purled or slipped stitches between the knitted stitches. Try going down a needle size or two when you experiment with your swatches.

SPROUTS

This pattern uses charts. If you're new to using charts, you'll soon discover they make your knitting easy and fun. Look in the Techniques chapter for some helpful hints on how to read charts.

FINISHED MEASUREMENTS

5.25" x 68"/13.5 cm x 172.5cm

YARN

Berroco Ultra Alpaca (50% superfine alpaca, 50% Peruvian wool; 215 yd/198m per 100g skein) (for substitution purposes, 20 sts/26 rows = 4"/10cm as per ball band)
- MC: #6273 Irwyn Green Mix; 2 skeins
- CC: #6201 Winter White; 2 skeins

Or approximately 235 yards each MC and CC of worsted weight alpaca blend yarn

NEEDLES & NOTIONS

1 US #4/3.5mm circular needle or 1 pair US #4/3.5mm straight needles
1 US #6/4mm circular needle
Tapestry needle

GAUGE

36 sts/22 rows = 4"/10cm in pattern stitch on larger needles, after blocking

Gauge notes: Remember that with double-knitting, you only see half the number of stitches as you look at one side of the double fabric. So to get 36 sts per 4"/10cm, you will see 18 sts on one side (the other 18 sts are on the other side).

Use your gauge swatch to work out what size needle will work for you for the cast-on and bind-off. The end of your swatch (and eventually your scarf) should be straight – neither flared nor pulled in.

PATTERN

With smaller needles and MC, cast on 51 sts.
Setup rows:
Row 1: With larger needles and MC, p1tbl, * k1, p1; rep from * to end.
Row 2: With CC, sl1 (a knit st), sl1 wyif (a purl st), * k1, sl1 wyif; rep from * to last st, sl1 wyib. Slide. On second pass, with MC, k1, p1, * sl1 wyib, p1; rep from * to last st, k1tbl. Turn. Begin the scarf by working Charts A & B as follows:

Chart A: Work odd rows only. On the row's first pass, with CC, sl edge st, then work row as charted to last st, sl1 wyib. Slide. On second pass, with MC, p edge st tbl, then work as charted. Note special instructions for Chart A lines 1 and 5: On the row's first pass, with CC, sl edge st, then work as charted to last 2 sts, sl1 wyib, sl1 wyif. Slide. On second pass, with MC, p edge st tbl, then work as charted to last 2 sts, k1, p1.

Chart B: Work even rows only. On the row's first pass, with CC, work row as charted to last edge st, sl1 wyif. Slide. On row's second pass, with MC, work the row as charted to last edge st, k1tbl.
Note special instructions for Chart B line 6: On the row's first pass, with CC, sl first st, sl1 wyif, then work as charted to last edge st, sl1 wyib. Slide. On second pass, with MC, k1, p1, then work as charted to last edge st, k1tbl.

When Chart B is complete, continue in solid color on either side of scarf as established for 57"/145 cm, from cast-on edge, or 11" less than desired finished length.

Work Charts C & D as follows:
Chart C: Work as for Chart A. Note special instructions for Chart C lines 67 and 73: On the row's first pass, with CC, sl edge st, then work as charted to last 2 sts, sl1 wyib, sl1 wyif. Slide. On second pass, with MC, p edge st tbl, then work as charted to last 2 sts, k1, p1.

Chart D: Work as for Chart B. Note special instructions for Chart D lines 68 and 72: On the row's first pass, with CC, sl first st, sl1 wyif, then work as charted to last edge st, sl1 wyib. Slide. On second pass, with MC, k1, p1, then work as charted to last edge st, k1tbl.

When Chart C is complete, work ending row: With MC, * k1, p1; rep from * to last st, k1.

Change to smaller needles and bind off as follows: K1 (edge st), k1, p1, pass first st over the next 2 sts, k1, pass first st over the next 2 sts, p1, pass first st over the next 2 sts, and continue in pattern until 2 sts remain. Pass the first st over the last st and pull the yarn tail through the last st to finish.

FINISHING

Weave in ends. Block scarf without stretching.

CHARTS FOR BEGINNING OF SCARF
For Chart A, work odd rows only. For Chart B, work even rows only.

CHART A

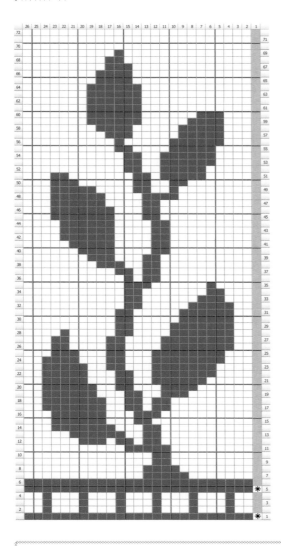

CHART B

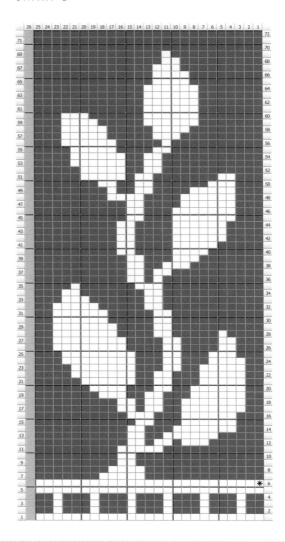

READING CHARTS

All rows of the charts are read right to left. When looking at the chart, think of each square that faces you as a knit stitch that has a buddy purl stitch on the opposite side. The buddy purl stitch comes right after its knit stitch on the needle. As you read the chart, you'll work the knit stitch (facing you) first, and then you'll work its buddy purl stitch. If the knit stitch facing you is in your working yarn color, then knit it and slip its buddy with the yarn in front. If the knit stitch is in the other color, slip it with the yarn in back, and purl its buddy.

For each row of the chart you will be making one pass with the contrasting color (CC), and then you will slide the stitches to the opposite end of your needle and make another pass of the same row in the main color (MC). At the end of the row, you will have formed the charted stitches on both the front and back of your work. When you turn your work, you'll see the buddy stitches that you purled become the knit stitches on the new side.

The edge stitch (shown in grey on the charts) is a single stitch, without a buddy, and is always worked with the MC.

This pattern uses four charts, two for the beginning of the scarf (A & B), and two for the opposite end (C & D). For each end, you'll use one chart for one side of your work

For Chart C, work odd rows only. For Chart D, work even rows only.

CHART C

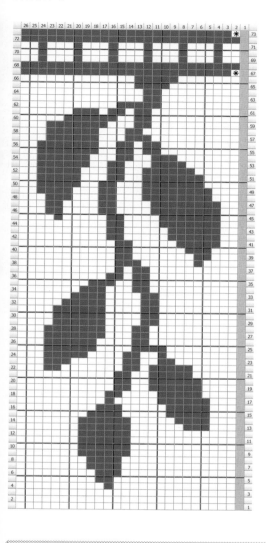

CHART D

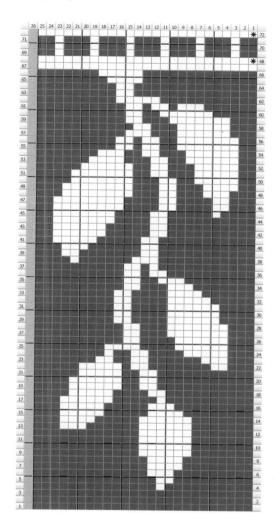

and the other chart for the second side of your work. Even though all the rows are shown on the charts, you'll work only the odd rows on Charts A & C and only the even rows on the opposite side, Charts B & D.

In order to maintain the edging, some rows have special instructions, indicated with an asterisk (*) on the charts. Look for them in the written notes.

A helpful tip: I suggest using a Post-it® note, magnetic strip, or colored tape above the line you're working. That way you can see the rows below, which helps you to "read" your knitting as you go. Keep in mind that you are working only the odd rows on the charts for one side, and only the even rows on the charts for the other side,

so move your place keeper up two rows on the chart to the next odd or even row.

KEY TO CHARTS

- ■ MC
- □ CC
- ▨ Edge stitch
- ✱ See written notes for special instructions

SURPRISE STRIPES

The surprise in this pattern becomes evident when you look at the stripes on one side… then turn it over. Magically, the stripes are vertical on one side and horizontal on the other!

FINISHED MEASUREMENTS
4.25" x 72"/11cm x 183cm

YARN
Rowan Calmer (75% cotton, 25% polyester; 175 yd/160m per 50g ball) (for substitution purposes, 21 sts/30 rows = 4"/10cm as per ball band)
- Color A: #460, Drift; 2 balls
- Color B: #476, Coral; 2 balls

Or approximately 270 yards of light worsted weight yarn for Color A and approximately 250 yards of light worsted weight yarn for Color B.

NEEDLES & NOTIONS
1 US #4/3.5mm circular needle
Tapestry needle

GAUGE
34 sts = 4"/10cm in pattern stitch, after blocking

Gauge notes: Remember that with double-knitting, you only see half the number of stitches as you look at one side of the double fabric. So to get 34 sts per 4"/10cm, you will see 17 sts on one side (the other 17 sts are on the other side).

Use your gauge swatch to work out what size needle will work for you for the cast-on and bind-off. The end of your swatch (and eventually your scarf) should be straight – neither flared nor pulled in.

PATTERN NOTES
Each time the two strands of yarn end up at the same edge, the instructions call for the two colors to be twisted to carry the old color up the work and to form a tidy edge.

Pattern stitch is a multiple of 4 sts + 3.

PATTERN
With Color A, cast on 35 sts.

Setup row: * K1, p1; rep from * to last st, k1. Slide.

Surprise Stripe Pattern:
Row 1: With Color B, k1, sl1 wyif, k1, * p1, k1, sl1 wyif, k1; rep from * to end. Turn.
Row 2: To twist the yarns and to carry Color A up the work, bring Color B toward the front of Color A, then under Color A, and then to the back; with Color B, p1, sl1 wyib, p1, * k1, p1, sl1 wyib, p1; rep from * to end. Slide.
Row 3: With Color A, p1, k1, p1, * sl1 wyib, p1, k1, p1; rep from * to end. Turn.
Row 4: To twist the yarns and to carry Color B up the work, bring Color A behind Color B, passing it under Color B, and then toward the front; with Color A, k1, p1, k1, * sl1 wyif, k1, p1, k1; rep from * to end. Slide.

Rep rows 1-4 until scarf measures approx 72"/183cm or desired length, ending with row 2. Turn.

Ending row: With Color A, p1, * k1, p1; rep from * to end.

Bind off as follows: With Color A, k1, p1, k1, pass first st over the next 2 sts, p1, pass first st over the next 2 sts, k1, pass first st over the next 2 sts, and continue in pattern until 2 sts remain. Pass the first st over the last st and pull the yarn tail through the last st.

FINISHING
Weave in ends. Block scarf.

MAKE IT YOUR OWN

Have fun trying highly contrasting yarns, tone on tone, a mix of textures such as mohair and plied, or multi-colored combined with solids.

You'll need to experiment with different needle sizes and adjust as needed for the fabric's thickness and getting squared ends in casting on and binding off.

Sometimes I like to use two different yarn weights, as in the Classic Shades sample. I wanted the worsted shaded yarn to be more prominent than the solid, so I used a DK weight for the white.

Yarns used:
- *Tone-on-tone (top right): Rowan Felted Tweed DK in Phantom (153) and Camel (157)*
- *Mohair and plied (middle right): Katia Ingenua in Celery (15) and Debbie Bliss Cashmerino DK in Ultramarine (36)*
- *Multi-colored and solid (below): Universal Yarn Classic Shades in Grapevine (711) and Debbie Bliss Cashmerino DK in White (02).*

CHAPTER 6: LUSCIOUS LACINESS

I love the delicate, airy look of lace. It can echo elegant traditions passed down through the centuries. Or it can offer a modern geometric twist. From easy-to-memorize stitch patterns to complex challenges, lace offers something for everyone.

FEATHER AND FAN

This revision of the popular Feather and Fan stitch pattern makes it the same on both sides.

FINISHED MEASUREMENTS
8" x 62"/20.5cm x 157.5cm

YARN
Rowan Kid Classic (70% lambswool, 26% kid mohair, 4% nylon; 153 yd/140m per 50g ball) (for substitution purposes, 23-25 sts = 4"/10cm as per ball band); color: #862, Teal; 2 balls.

Or approximately 265 yards of worsted weight yarn

NEEDLES & NOTIONS
1 pair US #8/5mm straight needles
Tapestry needle

GAUGE
19 sts = 4"/10cm in pattern stitch, after blocking

PATTERN NOTE
Pattern stitch is a multiple of 18 sts + 2.

PATTERN
Loosely cast on 38 sts.

Reversible Feather and Fan Pattern
Row 1: Knit.
Row 2: Knit.
Row 3: K1, * [k2tog] 3 times, [yo, k1] 6 times, [k2tog] 3 times; rep from * to last st, k1.

Rep rows 1-3 until scarf measures 62"/157.5cm or desired length.

Knit one row. Bind off loosely.

FINISHING
Weave in ends. Block scarf, stretching the knitting as you would for lace.

LILTING LEAVES

Typically, a leaf lace consists mostly of knit stitches on the right side, leaving an obvious "wrong" side on the other. Here I've re-invented the leaf pattern to include both knits and purls so one side's the same as the other.

FINISHED MEASUREMENTS
7" x 60"/18cm x 152.5cm

YARN
Classic Elite Yarns Fresco (60% wool, 30% baby alpaca, 10% angora; 164 yd/150m per 50g skein) (for substitution purposes, 26 sts = 4"/10cm as per ball band); color: #5315, Pea Pod; 3 skeins.

Or approximately 350 yards of sport weight yarn

Yarn Note: If you substitute yarns, choose one that can stand up to slight ironing. A gentle pressing is needed for the pattern to lie flat.

NEEDLES & NOTIONS
1 pair US #5/3.75mm straight needles
Tapestry needle

GAUGE
25 sts/32 rows = 4"/10cm in stockinette stitch

PATTERN NOTES
Cast on and bind off loosely to accommodate stretching when you block the lace. You may want to experiment with a swatch.

When the pattern calls for a yo before a purl stitch, be careful to bring the yarn all the way around your needle, or else no stitch will be formed.

There are five edge stitches on each side; they are included in both the charted and written instructions.

Pattern stitch is a multiple of 18 sts + 15, plus 10 edge sts (5 each side).

PATTERN
Loosely cast on 43 sts.

Setup rows:
Rows 1-3: Knit.
Row 4: K2, [yo, k2tog] 9 times, yo, k3tog, yo, [ssk, yo] nine times, k2.
Rows 5-7: Knit.
Row 8 (same as row 24 of chart): K5, p7, k8, p1, k2, p7, k13.

Leaf Lace Pattern
Work lace chart or follow written instructions below until scarf measures 60"/152.5cm or desired length.

Row 1: K2, yo, k2tog, k1, yo, p2tog, p5, k6, k2tog, yo, p1, k2, yo, p2tog, p5, k6, k2tog, yo, k1, ssk, yo, k2.
Row 2: K6, p6, k7, p2, k3, p6, k7, p1, k5.
Row 3: K2, yo, k2tog, k2, yo, p2tog, p4, k5, k2tog, yo, ssp, yo, k1, yo, ssk, yo, p2tog, p4, k5, k2tog, yo, p1, k1, ssk, yo, k2.
Row 4: K7, p5, k6, p3, k4, p5, k6, p2, k5.

Row 5: K2, yo, k2tog, k3, yo, p2tog, p3, k4, k2tog, yo, ssp, p1, [yo, k1] twice, ssk, yo, p2tog, p3, k4, k2tog, yo, p2, k1, ssk, yo, k2.
Row 6: K8, [p4, k5] 3 times, p3, k5.
Row 7: K2, yo, k2tog, k4, yo, p2tog, p2, k3, k2tog, yo, ssp, p2, yo, k1, yo, k2, ssk, yo, p2tog, p2, k3, k2tog, yo, p3, k1, ssk, yo, k2.
Row 8: K9, p3, k4, p5, k6, p3, k4, p4, k5.

Row 9: K2, yo, k2tog, k5, yo, p2tog, p1, k2, k2tog, yo, ssp, p3, yo, k1, yo, k3, ssk, yo, p2tog, p1, k2, k2tog, yo, p4, k1, ssk, yo, k2.
Row 10: K10, p2, k3, p6, k7, p2, k3, p5, k5.
Row 11: K2, yo, k2tog, k6, yo, p2tog, k1, k2tog, yo, ssp, p4, yo, k1, yo, k4, ssk, yo, p2tog, k1, k2tog, yo, p5, k1, ssk, yo, k2.
Row 12: K11, p1, k2, p7, k8, p1, k2, p6, k5.

Row 13: K2, yo, k2tog, k5, ssk, yo, p1, k2, yo, p2tog, p5, k6, ssk, yo, k3, yo, p2tog, p4, k1, ssk, yo, k2.
Row 14: Rep row 10.
Row 15: K2, yo, k2tog, k4, k2tog, yo, ssp, yo, k1, yo, ssk, yo, p2tog, p4, k5, k2tog, yo, ssp, yo, k1, yo, ssk, yo, p2tog, p3, k1, ssk, yo, k2.
Row 16: Rep row 8.

Row 17: K2, yo, k2tog, k3, k2tog, yo, ssp, p1, [yo, k1] twice, ssk, yo, p2tog, p3, k4, k2tog, yo, ssp, p1, [yo, k1] twice, ssk, yo, p2tog, p2, k1, ssk, yo, k2.
Row 18: Rep row 6.
Row 19: K2, yo, k2tog, k2, k2tog, yo, ssp, p2, yo, k1, yo, k2, ssk, yo, p2tog, p2, k3, k2tog, yo, ssp, p2, yo, k1, yo, k2, ssk, yo, p2tog,

p1, k1, ssk, yo, k2.
Row 20: Rep row 4.

Row 21: K2, yo, k2tog, k1, k2tog, yo, ssp, p3, yo, k1, yo, k3, ssk,
yo, p2tog, p1, k2, k2tog, yo, ssp, p3, yo, k1, yo, k3, ssk, yo, p2tog,
k1, ssk, yo, k2.
Row 22: Rep row 2.
Row 23: K2, yo, [k2tog] twice, yo, ssp, p4, yo, k1, yo, k4, ssk, yo,
p2tog, k1, k2tog, yo, ssp, p4, yo, k1, yo, k4, ssk, yo, p2tog, ssk,
yo, k2.
Row 24: K5, p7, k8, p1, k2, p7, k13.
Rep rows 1-24.

Ending rows:
Rows 1-3: Knit.
Row 4: K2, [yo, k2tog 9 times, yo, k3tog, yo, [ssk, yo] 9 times,
k2.
Rows 5-7: Knit.

Bind off loosely.

FINISHING

Weave in ends. Block scarf, stretching the knitting as you
would for lace. Gently press to eliminate the ridges formed
by the knit and purl sides of the pattern's leaf shapes.

VARIATION

Use fingering weight yarn and add additional stitch pattern
repeats for a very delicate look.

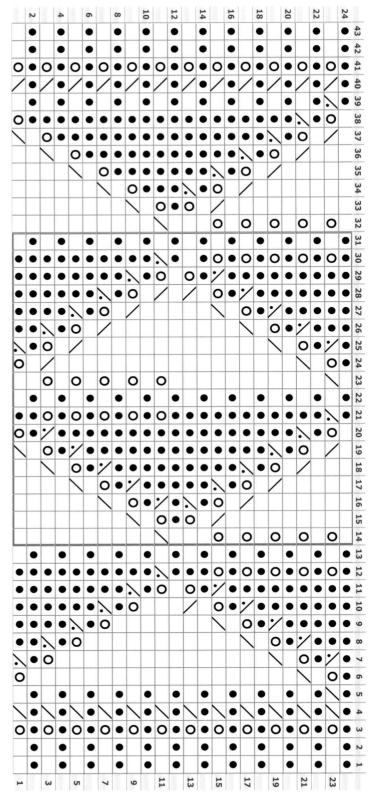

KEY TO CHART

Knit
Yo
Purl
P2tog
K2tog
Ssk
Ssp

STEFANIE MOEBIUS

I learned this intriguing moebius construction from Cat Bordhi. Not only does it have no "right" side, it is an endless loop. The pattern evolves from the cast-on in the center to the outer edge. The optional contrasting color for the edging helps to accentuate the moebius's infinite edge. The cast-on may be a bit tricky to learn, but it's well worth the effort.

FINISHED MEASUREMENTS

34"/86.5cm circumference x 15"/38cm width

YARN

Lorna's Laces Shepherd Sport (100% superwash wool; 200 yds/183m per 70g skein) (for substitution purposes, 6 sts = 1"/2.5cm as per ball band)
- MC: The Bean; 3 skeins
  Or approximately 450 yards of sport weight yarn
- CC (optional): Grand Street Ink; 1 skein
  Or approximately 65 yards of sport weight yarn

NEEDLES & NOTIONS

1 US #5/3.75mm circular needle, 47"/120cm
Locking stitch markers for keeping track of cast-on sts (optional)
1 stitch marker in Color A for marking BOR
16 stitch markers in Color B for marking repeats (optional)
Tapestry needle

GAUGE

19 sts = 4"/10cm in Diamond Stitch Pattern

PATTERN NOTES

The Moebius Cast-On uses a special technique that you can find on page 14 of the Techniques chapter.

Unlike most cast-ons, this Moebius Cast-On should be worked quite firmly to avoid loose sts in the center of your work.

I like to place locking stitch markers every 50 sts as I count the cast-on sts so that I don't have to count large numbers of sts over and over. The locking markers are typically large enough that they won't fall through the needle-side, yarnover-style cast-on sts. Remove these markers once you've determined that you have the correct number of cast-on sts.

As you work the first round, I highly recommend placing a small stitch marker every 20 sts. This will make it much

easier to find mistakes. Make sure the markers for the repeats are a different color than the BOR marker.

If you're new to using charts, you'll find helpful hints in the Techniques chapter.

BOR = beginning of round.

PATTERN

With MC and using the special Moebius Cast-On given in the Techniques chapter, cast on 160 sts (not including slip knot). Place the Color A stitch marker on right-hand needle to mark beginning of round.

Starting with the slip knot stitch, as described in Moebius Cast-On, begin Diamond Stitch Pattern. I recommend placing a Color B marker every 20 sts, between every 2 repeats.

Diamond Stitch Pattern (multiple of 10 sts)
Work Chart A or follow line-by-line instructions below:
Rnd 1 and all odd-numbered rnds: Purl.
Rnd 2: * K3, k2tog, yo, k1, yo, k2tog, k2; rep from * to end.
Rnd 4: * K2, k2tog, yo, k3, yo, k2tog, k1; rep from * to end.
Rnd 6: * K1, k2tog, yo, k5, yo, k2tog; rep from * to end.
Rnd 8: * K1, yo, k2tog, k5, k2tog, yo; rep from * to end.
Rnd 10: * K2, yo, k2tog, k3, k2tog, yo, k1; rep from * to end.
Rnd 12: * K3, yo, k2tog, k1, k2tog, yo, k2; rep from * to end.
Repeat Rnds 1-12 five more times for a total of six repeats.
(Because the repeats fall both above and below the cast-on round, the six repeats will show as twelve across the width of the moebius when completed.)

Edging
Work Chart B or follow line-by-line instructions below:
Rnd 1: With MC, purl.
Rnd 2: * K3, k2tog, yo, k1, yo, k2tog, k2; rep from * to end.
Rnd 3: Purl.
Rnd 4: Knit.
Rnd 5: If using optional CC, break MC yarn and with CC, * K1, p1; rep from * to end.
Rnd 6: Knit.
Rnd 7: Purl.
Rnd 8: * K2tog, yo; rep from * to end.

Rnd 9: Purl.
Rnd 10: Knit.
Rnd 11: Purl.

Loosely bind off knitwise.

FINISHING
Weave in ends.

Blocking a moebius can be tricky. In her books, Cat Bordhi recommends folding a towel, placing it on an ironing board, and draping the scarf over that, rotating it so that all the surfaces lie flat at some point.

Rather than wet blocking, I suggest spritzing the sections on top of the board with water as you go. Otherwise, the weight of wet knitting hanging down may stretch the piece. Or if you're like me and like to use blocking boards, you can block one third of it at a time, turning it before it is dry to prevent creasing. With this method, you can either wet block or spritz.

CHART A (DIAMOND PATTERN)

10	9	8	7	6	5	4	3	2	1	
		O	/		/	O				12
•	•	•	•	•	•	•	•	•	•	11
	O	/				/	O			10
•	•	•	•	•	•	•	•	•	•	9
O	/						/	O		8
•	•	•	•	•	•	•	•	•	•	7
/	O					O	/			6
•	•	•	•	•	•	•	•	•	•	5
	/	O			O	/				4
•	•	•	•	•	•	•	•	•	•	3
		/	O		O	/				2
•	•	•	•	•	•	•	•	•	•	1

CHART B (EDGING)
If using contrasting color for edging, start it on Round 5.

10	9	8	7	6	5	4	3	2	1	
•	•	•	•	•	•	•	•	•	•	11
										10
•	•	•	•	•	•	•	•	•	•	9
O	/	O	/	O	/	O	/	O	/	8
•	•	•	•	•	•	•	•	•	•	7
										6
	•		•		•		•			5
										4
•	•	•	•	•	•	•	•	•	•	3
		/	O		O	/				2
•	•	•	•	•	•	•	•	•	•	1

KEY TO CHARTS

•	purl
☐	knit
/	k2tog
O	yo

MAKE IT YOUR OWN

Most lace patterns have a definite right and wrong side. There are several ways to transform them to be reversible. If the stitch pattern has an even number of rows, either add or subtract a row to make an odd number. I did this with the Feather and Fan scarf (see page 113).

Another technique is to work some sections of the pattern in knit, and others in purl. You can see how I applied this method to the leaf motif in the Lilting Leaves pattern (page 115).

A third option is to use a stitch pattern that adapts well to garter stitch, like the diamond design in the Stefanie Moebius (page 119).

The key to altering lace patterns is to swatch, swatch, and swatch. For me, this is half the fun as I discover unexpected ways to achieve unique results.

Oh yes, and one other hint that I learned the hard way... you might want write your stitch pattern alterations as you go! Especially with lace, it can be hard to re-invent your creation after the fact.

When you're all done experimenting, you'll have your own lacey stitch pattern that you can apply to any scarf shape you like.

TUMBLING BLOCKS

This super easy pattern is worked lengthwise and lends itself to a wide variety of yarn weights.

FINISHED MEASUREMENTS
6" x 72"/15cm x 183cm

YARN
Berroco Vintage DK (50% acrylic, 40% wool, 10% nylon; 288 yd/263m per 100g skein) (for substitution purposes, 22 sts/28 rows = 4"/10cm as per ball band); color: #2167, Dewberry; 2 skeins.

Or approximately 380 yards of dk weight yarn

NEEDLES & NOTIONS
1 US #7/4.5mm circular needle, 60"/150cm 1 US #8/5mm straight needle (optional for bind-off)
Tapestry needle

GAUGE
20 sts = 4"/10cm in garter stitch or Tumbling Blocks pattern, after blocking

PATTERN NOTES
Scarf is worked lengthwise.

When you make the gauge swatch, it's the perfect time to choose the cast-on you want to use and to estimate the yardage you'll need if you choose the long-tail method.

You may want to use your gauge swatch to explore using one size larger needle for the bind-off.

Refer to the Techniques chapter, page 12, for suggestions for working lengthwise scarves.

Tumbling Blocks Pattern is a multiple of 20 sts + 1.

PATTERN
Very loosely cast on 361 sts.

Knit one row.

Tumbling Blocks Pattern
Rows 1, 3, 5, 7, 9 and 11 (RS): * [Ssk, yo] 5 times, k10: rep from * to last st, k1.
Row 2 and all even rows: Knit.
Rows 13, 15, 17, 19, 21, and 23: K1, * k10, [yo, k2tog] 5 times; rep from * to end.
Row 24: Knit.
Rep rows 1-24 once more.

Bind off very loosely, using larger needle if desired.

FINISHING
Weave in ends. Block, pinning out angles.

THAT'S A WRAP

Many scarf patterns translate well into wraps. You can easily make a pattern wider and longer by adding additional stitch pattern repeats. You can also play with yarn weights and needles sizes. Maybe some lace yarn on larger needles? A medium weight pattern made bold by using bulky yarn? I hope you enjoy making your own wraps as much as I do. It's an easy way to create a unique wardrobe accessory.

Here, I used a scarf pattern's basics to create a wrap. Where the Feather and Fan scarf pattern (page 113) calls for two pattern repeats, I used 16 repeats to form the width of this wrap.

I also wanted a completely different look, so I used the sparkly Blue Heron Rayon Metallic yarn instead of the scarf version's mohair.

This wrap used about 975 yards on a size US7/3.5mm, 47"/120cm circular needle. Instead of casting on 38 stitches for the scarf, I cast on 290 stitches.

If you'd like to make this wrap yourself, aim for a gauge of about 22 stitches per 4"/10cm in stockinette stitch. The Feather and Fan Wrap works up to about 64"/162.5cm x 24"/61cm.

STANDARD ABBREVIATIONS

approx	approximately
BOR	beginning of round
CC	contrasting color
cm	centimeter[s]
dec	decrease[ing]
dpn[s]	double pointed needles[s]
g	grams
inc	increase[ing]
k	knit
k1tbl	knit the next st through the back loop
k2tog	knit two together
k3tog	knit three together
kfb	knit into front and back of stitch
m	meter[s]
MC	main color
m1	Make 1 stitch: Insert left needle, from front to back, under strand of yarn which runs between last stitch on left needle and first stitch on right needle; knit this stitch through back loop. 1 stitch increased.
mm	millimeter[s]
oz	ounces
p	purl
p2tog	purl two together
PM	place marker
psso	pass slipped stitch[es] over
p1tbl	purl the next st through the back loop
rep	repeat
RS	right side[s]
rnd[s]	round[s]
SK2P	slip 1 stitch knitwise, knit two together, pass slipped stitch over
S2KP2	slip next 2 sts together, knitwise, as if to work a k2tog. Knit next st, then pass both slipped sts together over st just knit. This forms a centered double decrease.
SSK	slip next 2 sts knitwise, one at a time, to right needle. Insert tip of left needle, from left to right, into the fronts of these 2 sts; knit them together from this position.
SSP	slip next 2 sts knitwise, one at a time, to right needle. Slip them both, purlwise, back to left needle. Purl them together through their back loops.
sl	slip
slide	Slide stitches to opposite end of needle and do not turn work.
st[s]	stitch[es]
tbl	through back of loop[s]
WS	wrong side[s]
wyif	with yarn in front
wyib	with yarn in back
yd	yard[s]
yo	yarn over
*	repeat directions after * as indicated
[ ]	repeat directions within brackets as many times as indicated

REFERENCES

CHAPTER 2: SURPRISINGLY SIMPLE STITCHES

- Allen, Pam. Knitting for Dummies. Wiley Publishing, 2002. P. 39.
- Epstein, Nicky. Knitting on the Edge: Ribs, Ruffles, Lace, Fringes, Floral, Points and Picots. Sixth&Spring Books, 2004. P. 148.
- Walker, Barbara G. A Treasury of Knitting Patterns. Schoolhouse Press, 1998. Pp. 11, 34-35.

CHAPTER 3: MULTI-YARN MARVELS

- Neighbors, Jane F. Reversible Two-Color Knitting. Charles Scribner Sons, 1974. P. 18.
- Radcliffe, Margaret. The Essential Guide to Color Knitting Techniques. Storey Publishing, 2008.
- Wiseman, Nancie M., The Knitter's Book of Finishing Techniques. Martingale & Company, 2002. P. 14.

CHAPTER 4: CABLES AND RIBS IN REVERSE

- 99 Knit Stitches. (Booklet #2973.) Leisure Arts, 1997. P. 24.
- Chin, Lily M. Power Cables: The Ultimate Guide to Knitting Inventive Cables. Interweave Press, 2010.
- The Harmony Guides. Vol. 2: 450 Knitting Stitches. Collins & Brown, 2004. P. 70.
- ———. Vol. 3: 440 More Knitting Stitches. Collins & Brown, 2004. P. 37.
- ———. Vol. 5: 220 Aran Stitches. Collins & Brown, 2004. P. 18.
- Walker, Barbara G. A Second Treasury of Knitting Patterns. Schoolhouse Press, 1998. P. 147.

CHAPTER 5: TWICE THE FUN WITH DOUBLE-KNITTING

- Neighbors, Jane F. Reversible Two-Color Knitting. Charles Scribner Sons, 1974. Pp. 55, 112, 180, 182.

CHAPTER 6: LUSCIOUS LACE

- Bordhi, Cat. A Second Treasury of Magical Knitting. Passing Paws Press, 2005.
- Bordhi, Cat. "Intro to Moebius Knitting." YouTube. 2007. http://www.youtube.com/watch?v=LVnTda7F2V4.
- Knight, Erika, ed. The Harmony Guides: Lace & Eyelets. Interweave Press, 2007. Pp. 88, 181.
- Walker, Barbara. A Second Treasury of Knitting Patterns. Schoolhouse Press, 1998. P. 263

SPECIAL TECHNIQUES

- Chin, Lily. Lily Chin's Knitting Tips & Tricks: Shortcuts and Techniques Every Knitter Should Know. Potter Craft, 2009.
- Stitch Diva Studios. Online tutorial. "Knitting On, Purling On - Cast On." http://www.stitchdiva.com/tutorials/knitting/knit-on-purl-on.
- Swanson, Meg. "Knitted-On Cast On" and "Austrian Variation: Plus K & P Cast On." In The Best of Vogue Knitting. Sixth & Spring Books, 2007. Pp. 78-79.
- Watson, Virginia. eHow online tutorial. "How to Determine the Length of Yarn for Knitting Cast On." 2010. http://www.ehow.com/how_7701638_determine-length-yarn-knitting-cast.html.
- Wiseman, Nancie M. The Knitter's Book of Finishing Techniques. Martingale & Co., 2002. P. 14.

RESOURCES

GRAPH PAPER

If you use conventional graph paper, the squares are too tall for knit stitches and your pattern will appear more elongated than what you will see when you translate it to yarn. Notice that the gauge for most yarns shows more rows per inch than stitches per inch. This means that the stitch height is shorter than the stitch width, so there will be more rows than stitch per inch.

To print graph paper appropriate for knitting charts from the web:
- http://www.theknittingsite.com/graph.htm
- http://www.printablepaper.net/category/knitting
- http://www.knitonthenet.com/designchart/

Or try graph paper generating software:
- http://www.knittingsoftware.com/printagridnewweb.htm
- http://www.knitpicks.com/Print-A-Grid_AD80153.html

KNITTING SOFTWARE

Knit Visualizer http://www.knitfoundry.com/software.html
Swatch Wizard http://www.knittingsoftware.com/pswatchwizard/swatchwiz.htm
Stitch & Motif Maker http://www.knittingsoftware.com/stitchmotif.htm

YARN STORES & YARN COMPANIES

Angelika's (online)
Ball & Skein & More (Cambria, California)
Berroco Cast On Café (Willoughby, Ohio)
Colorful Stitches (online)
Heavenly Hues Yarn (online)
ImagiKnit (San Francisco, California)
Jimmy Beans (online)
Knit Picks (online)
Knit Purl (Portland, Oregon)
Michael's (Paso Robles, California)
Monarch Knitting & Quilts (Pacific Grove, California)
Mountain Colors Nestucca Bay Yarns (online)
Paradise Fibers (online)
Ranch Dog Knitting (Atascadero, California)
The Scarlet Skein (Paso Robles, California)
WEBS (online)
Yarnmarket (online and Pickerington, OH)

ACKNOWLEDGMENTS

It amazes me to look back and realize how many people helped out with this book, both directly and indirectly. I give them my warmest thanks!

First, the dear friend who started it all… I want to thank Margaret Harper for her enthusiasm and friendship. She not only re-awakened my childhood interest in knitting, but offered her support and great sense of humor. She taught me about knitting, life, and being a friend. My brother, Rick, insisted I follow my heart, and made it possible to proceed against some serious odds. Mary Joyce has been a great influence on me since the first grade, and lent her artistic input to the book. And my husband, Steve, has been understanding of my obsessive work and clacking needles. I think I last cooked for him about three years ago, and he hasn't complained even once. (Hmm.) I give all of you my love and gratitude.

Special friends who were involved early on include the amazing Alana Dakos, who has taught me so much over the years and lent her great sense of style to my early design process. Her "Never Not Knitting" designs and podcast continue to entertain and inspire me. Also, the wonderful knitter and column writer Jack Lewis encouraged me to write my very first pattern, and remains a supportive email buddy to this day. Alex Badasci, with his Studio Creek Web Design, set up my web site, helps with marketing, and gave me a good "platform" to leap from.

My local yarn shops, their owners, and my fellow knitters there offered all kinds of camaraderie and advice throughout the writing of this book. And yarn. Lots and lots of yarn.

I consider my tech editors to be nothing short of miracle workers. Elizabeth Sullivan's thorough expertise touches every page of this book. Tana Pageler worked diligently to polish several of the patterns. Their expertise and advice have been invaluable. Elizabeth Green Musselman had the daunting task of editing the book; her keen eye and attention to detail improved the original manuscript in countless ways.

I'm extremely grateful to the knitters who made my patterns come alive by testing and sample knitting. How lucky I've been to work with you all! Thank you to: Eliana Bahri, Kristina Bird, Patricia Bishop, Toni Blye, Christy Chapman, Alana Dakos, Cindy Drozynski, Barb Kervin, Anne Lustig, Deborah Lynch, Kristie Naranjo, Michelle Ogden, JoAnn Pedersen, Dawn Penny, Meg Prescott, Shirley Robb, Andrea Sanchez, Jody Lee Strine, and Donna Warnell.

For its part in shaping my knowledge base, I want to thank The Knitting Guild Association. I learned so much working on Level 1 of the Master Hand Knitting program, and I continue to enjoy the learning and friendships in the local Guilds I belong to – the SLO Knitting Guild of San Luis Obispo, California, and the Northcoast Knitting Guild in Northeast Ohio. I appreciate the dedication of the volunteers who keep the local guilds vibrant.

Finally, I want to thank Shannon Okey for the opportunity to originally publish this book.

ABOUT THE AUTHOR

Audrey Knight is known in the online knitting community as AudKnits. She has contributed designs to Knitty, Knotions and the 2010 Knitting Pattern-a-Day Calendar. She is also honored to be part of the Knit Picks Independent Designer Program. Her patterns, blog, tips, and techniques can be found at AudKnits.com.